C-4306   CAREER EXAMINATION SERIES

This is your
PASSBOOK for...

Credentialing Specialist

Test Preparation Study Guide
Questions & Answers

NATIONAL LEARNING CORPORATION®

COPYRIGHT NOTICE

This book is SOLELY intended for, is sold ONLY to, and its use is RESTRICTED to individual, bona fide applicants or candidates who qualify by virtue of having seriously filed applications for appropriate license, certificate, professional and/or promotional advancement, higher school matriculation, scholarship, or other legitimate requirements of education and/or governmental authorities.

This book is NOT intended for use, class instruction, tutoring, training, duplication, copying, reprinting, excerption, or adaptation, etc., by:

1) Other publishers
2) Proprietors and/or Instructors of "Coaching" and/or Preparatory Courses
3) Personnel and/or Training Divisions of commercial, industrial, and governmental organizations
4) Schools, colleges, or universities and/or their departments and staffs, including teachers and other personnel
5) Testing Agencies or Bureaus
6) Study groups which seek by the purchase of a single volume to copy and/or duplicate and/or adapt this material for use by the group as a whole without having purchased individual volumes for each of the members of the group
7) Et al.

Such persons would be in violation of appropriate Federal and State statutes.

PROVISION OF LICENSING AGREEMENTS – Recognized educational, commercial, industrial, and governmental institutions and organizations, and others legitimately engaged in educational pursuits, including training, testing, and measurement activities, may address request for a licensing agreement to the copyright owners, who will determine whether, and under what conditions, including fees and charges, the materials in this book may be used them. In other words, a licensing facility exists for the legitimate use of the material in this book on other than an individual basis. However, it is asseverated and affirmed here that the material in this book CANNOT be used without the receipt of the express permission of such a licensing agreement from the Publishers. Inquiries re licensing should be addressed to the company, attention rights and permissions department.

All rights reserved, including the right of reproduction in whole or in part, in any form or by any means, electronic or mechanical, including photocopying, recording, or by any information storage and retrieval system, without permission in writing from the Publisher.

Copyright © 2024 by
National Learning Corporation

212 Michael Drive, Syosset, NY 11791
(516) 921-8888 • www.passbooks.com
E-mail: info@passbooks.com

PASSBOOK® SERIES

THE *PASSBOOK® SERIES* has been created to prepare applicants and candidates for the ultimate academic battlefield – the examination room.

At some time in our lives, each and every one of us may be required to take an examination – for validation, matriculation, admission, qualification, registration, certification, or licensure.

Based on the assumption that every applicant or candidate has met the basic formal educational standards, has taken the required number of courses, and read the necessary texts, the *PASSBOOK® SERIES* furnishes the one special preparation which may assure passing with confidence, instead of failing with insecurity. Examination questions – together with answers – are furnished as the basic vehicle for study so that the mysteries of the examination and its compounding difficulties may be eliminated or diminished by a sure method.

This book is meant to help you pass your examination provided that you qualify and are serious in your objective.

The entire field is reviewed through the huge store of content information which is succinctly presented through a provocative and challenging approach – the question-and-answer method.

A climate of success is established by furnishing the correct answers at the end of each test.

You soon learn to recognize types of questions, forms of questions, and patterns of questioning. You may even begin to anticipate expected outcomes.

You perceive that many questions are repeated or adapted so that you can gain acute insights, which may enable you to score many sure points.

You learn how to confront new questions, or types of questions, and to attack them confidently and work out the correct answers.

You note objectives and emphases, and recognize pitfalls and dangers, so that you may make positive educational adjustments.

Moreover, you are kept fully informed in relation to new concepts, methods, practices, and directions in the field.

You discover that you are actually taking the examination all the time: you are preparing for the examination by "taking" an examination, not by reading extraneous and/or supererogatory textbooks.

In short, this PASSBOOK®, used directedly, should be an important factor in helping you to pass your test.

CREDENTIALING SPECIALIST

DESCRIPTION:
Credential and re-credential various providers, including physicians, healthcare delivery organizations, or pharmacies, according to applicable specifications; maintain and update credentialing database; assist with coordinating credentialing committee; process, track and file credentialing applications within established standards; respond to internal and external customer inquiries regarding credentialing status.

DISTINGUISHING FEATURES OF THE CLASS:
Under the direction of the Program Administrator, an incumbent of this class is responsible for providing administrative support for the process of privileging and credentialing the medical staff at the Medical Center. Performing primary source verification and ensuring that all physicians, residents, fellows, dentists, and allied health professionals are clinically qualified for the privileges applied for are major responsibilities of this position. Work is performed in compliance with detailed requirements, guidelines, and deadlines specified by the Joint Commission (JCAHO), Centers for Medicare & Medicaid Services (CMS), the National Committee for Quality Assurance (NCQA), State Education Department, Health Department, and the Hospital Board. Supervision is exercised over a number of clerical and office support staff. Does related work as required.

EXAMPLES OF DUTIES:
- Processes providers credentialing and re-credentialing applications:
- Monitors the status of applications and follows up as needed through completion;
- Compiles and maintains copies of current state licenses/registrations, DEA certificates, malpractice coverage and any other required credentialing documents for providers;
- Maintains credential files for each member of the medical-dental staff and ensures provider information is current;
- Enters provider information into credentialing software;
- Scans credentialing information into appropriate provider electronic profiles;
- Tracks license and certification expirations for providers to ensure timely renewal;
- Acts as a liaison between the Credentialing Department and hospital departments and other internal and external customers;
- Participates in the development and revision of policies and procedures for credentialing, quality assurance, professional standards and administrative functions;
- Participates in performance improvement projects relative to the quality of service;
- Assists with the analysis of clinical practice of medical-dental staff members;
- Maintains related records and prepares reports;
- Participates in meetings, committees, seminars, workshops and professional affiliations with flexibility to attend evening meetings.

- Performs primary source verification of professional education, training and employment, clinical licensure, board certifications, Drug Enforcement Administration (DEA) registration and infection control and other relevant certificates;
- Queries National Practitioner Database (NPDB) and other relevant national databases and organizations, conducts references checks, and malpractice audit history;
- Requests documentation, follows up on receipt of required documents, reviews documentation, and updates status of application to completion;
- Supports medical staff committees in the application and credentialing;
- Develops and maintains an Excel database for tracking sensitive documents, and monitoring expiring licenses and communication of required approvals;
- Compiles statistical information and data on medical staff and allied health professionals;
- Responds to requests for practitioner information regarding privileges;
- Participates in monthly committee meetings and training sessions for clinical department administrators;
- Accesses protected health information (PHI) in accordance with departmental assignments and guidelines defining levels of access (i.e. incidental vs. extensive);
- Uses computer applications or other automated systems such as spreadsheets, word processing, calendar, e-mail and database software in performing work assignments; May perform other incidental tasks, as needed.

REQUIRED KNOWLEDGE, SKILLS, ABILITIES AND ATTRIBUTES

Knowledge of medical staff credentialing processes, procedures and resources; knowledge of requirements of various organizations which affect the credentialing process such as JCAHO, CMS, NCQA, Education Department, Health Department; knowledge of the requirements of the Medical Center bylaws and policies regarding credentialing and privileging standards for the various clinical departments and sections; knowledge of medical terminology; ability to assemble and organize data; ability to determine priorities and meet deadlines; ability to effectively use computer applications such as spreadsheets, word processing, calendar, e-mail and database software in performing work assignments; ability to communicate effectively both orally and in writing; ability to establish and maintain effective working relationships with professional medical, technical, managerial, clerical and unskilled personnel; attention to detail; sound and mature judgment; flexibility; resourcefulness; initiative; tact; physical condition commensurate with the demands of the position.

HOW TO TAKE A TEST

I. YOU MUST PASS AN EXAMINATION

A. *WHAT EVERY CANDIDATE SHOULD KNOW*

Examination applicants often ask us for help in preparing for the written test. What can I study in advance? What kinds of questions will be asked? How will the test be given? How will the papers be graded?

As an applicant for a civil service examination, you may be wondering about some of these things. Our purpose here is to suggest effective methods of advance study and to describe civil service examinations.

Your chances for success on this examination can be increased if you know how to prepare. Those "pre-examination jitters" can be reduced if you know what to expect. You can even experience an adventure in good citizenship if you know why civil service exams are given.

B. *WHY ARE CIVIL SERVICE EXAMINATIONS GIVEN?*

Civil service examinations are important to you in two ways. As a citizen, you want public jobs filled by employees who know how to do their work. As a job seeker, you want a fair chance to compete for that job on an equal footing with other candidates. The best-known means of accomplishing this two-fold goal is the competitive examination.

Exams are widely publicized throughout the nation. They may be administered for jobs in federal, state, city, municipal, town or village governments or agencies.

Any citizen may apply, with some limitations, such as the age or residence of applicants. Your experience and education may be reviewed to see whether you meet the requirements for the particular examination. When these requirements exist, they are reasonable and applied consistently to all applicants. Thus, a competitive examination may cause you some uneasiness now, but it is your privilege and safeguard.

C. *HOW ARE CIVIL SERVICE EXAMS DEVELOPED?*

Examinations are carefully written by trained technicians who are specialists in the field known as "psychological measurement," in consultation with recognized authorities in the field of work that the test will cover. These experts recommend the subject matter areas or skills to be tested; only those knowledges or skills important to your success on the job are included. The most reliable books and source materials available are used as references. Together, the experts and technicians judge the difficulty level of the questions.

Test technicians know how to phrase questions so that the problem is clearly stated. Their ethics do not permit "trick" or "catch" questions. Questions may have been tried out on sample groups, or subjected to statistical analysis, to determine their usefulness.

Written tests are often used in combination with performance tests, ratings of training and experience, and oral interviews. All of these measures combine to form the best-known means of finding the right person for the right job.

II. HOW TO PASS THE WRITTEN TEST

A. NATURE OF THE EXAMINATION

To prepare intelligently for civil service examinations, you should know how they differ from school examinations you have taken. In school you were assigned certain definite pages to read or subjects to cover. The examination questions were quite detailed and usually emphasized memory. Civil service exams, on the other hand, try to discover your present ability to perform the duties of a position, plus your potentiality to learn these duties. In other words, a civil service exam attempts to predict how successful you will be. Questions cover such a broad area that they cannot be as minute and detailed as school exam questions.

In the public service similar kinds of work, or positions, are grouped together in one "class." This process is known as *position-classification*. All the positions in a class are paid according to the salary range for that class. One class title covers all of these positions, and they are all tested by the same examination.

B. FOUR BASIC STEPS

1) Study the announcement

How, then, can you know what subjects to study? Our best answer is: "Learn as much as possible about the class of positions for which you've applied." The exam will test the knowledge, skills and abilities needed to do the work.

Your most valuable source of information about the position you want is the official exam announcement. This announcement lists the training and experience qualifications. Check these standards and apply only if you come reasonably close to meeting them.

The brief description of the position in the examination announcement offers some clues to the subjects which will be tested. Think about the job itself. Review the duties in your mind. Can you perform them, or are there some in which you are rusty? Fill in the blank spots in your preparation.

Many jurisdictions preview the written test in the exam announcement by including a section called "Knowledge and Abilities Required," "Scope of the Examination," or some similar heading. Here you will find out specifically what fields will be tested.

2) Review your own background

Once you learn in general what the position is all about, and what you need to know to do the work, ask yourself which subjects you already know fairly well and which need improvement. You may wonder whether to concentrate on improving your strong areas or on building some background in your fields of weakness. When the announcement has specified "some knowledge" or "considerable knowledge," or has used adjectives like "beginning principles of…" or "advanced … methods," you can get a clue as to the number and difficulty of questions to be asked in any given field. More questions, and hence broader coverage, would be included for those subjects which are more important in the work. Now weigh your strengths and weaknesses against the job requirements and prepare accordingly.

3) Determine the level of the position

Another way to tell how intensively you should prepare is to understand the level of the job for which you are applying. Is it the entering level? In other words, is this the position in which beginners in a field of work are hired? Or is it an intermediate or advanced level? Sometimes this is indicated by such words as "Junior" or "Senior" in the class title. Other jurisdictions use Roman numerals to designate the level – Clerk I, Clerk II, for example. The word "Supervisor" sometimes appears in the title. If the level is not indicated by the title, check the description of duties. Will you be working under very close supervision, or will you have responsibility for independent decisions in this work?

4) Choose appropriate study materials

Now that you know the subjects to be examined and the relative amount of each subject to be covered, you can choose suitable study materials. For beginning level jobs, or even advanced ones, if you have a pronounced weakness in some aspect of your training, read a modern, standard textbook in that field. Be sure it is up to date and has general coverage. Such books are normally available at your library, and the librarian will be glad to help you locate one. For entry-level positions, questions of appropriate difficulty are chosen – neither highly advanced questions, nor those too simple. Such questions require careful thought but not advanced training.

If the position for which you are applying is technical or advanced, you will read more advanced, specialized material. If you are already familiar with the basic principles of your field, elementary textbooks would waste your time. Concentrate on advanced textbooks and technical periodicals. Think through the concepts and review difficult problems in your field.

These are all general sources. You can get more ideas on your own initiative, following these leads. For example, training manuals and publications of the government agency which employs workers in your field can be useful, particularly for technical and professional positions. A letter or visit to the government department involved may result in more specific study suggestions, and certainly will provide you with a more definite idea of the exact nature of the position you are seeking.

III. KINDS OF TESTS

Tests are used for purposes other than measuring knowledge and ability to perform specified duties. For some positions, it is equally important to test ability to make adjustments to new situations or to profit from training. In others, basic mental abilities not dependent on information are essential. Questions which test these things may not appear as pertinent to the duties of the position as those which test for knowledge and information. Yet they are often highly important parts of a fair examination. For very general questions, it is almost impossible to help you direct your study efforts. What we can do is to point out some of the more common of these general abilities needed in public service positions and describe some typical questions.

1) General information

Broad, general information has been found useful for predicting job success in some kinds of work. This is tested in a variety of ways, from vocabulary lists to questions about current events. Basic background in some field of work, such as sociology or economics, may be sampled in a group of questions. Often these are principles which have become familiar to most persons through exposure rather than through formal training. It is difficult to advise you how to study for these questions; being alert to the world around you is our best suggestion.

2) Verbal ability

An example of an ability needed in many positions is verbal or language ability. Verbal ability is, in brief, the ability to use and understand words. Vocabulary and grammar tests are typical measures of this ability. Reading comprehension or paragraph interpretation questions are common in many kinds of civil service tests. You are given a paragraph of written material and asked to find its central meaning.

3) Numerical ability
Number skills can be tested by the familiar arithmetic problem, by checking paired lists of numbers to see which are alike and which are different, or by interpreting charts and graphs. In the latter test, a graph may be printed in the test booklet which you are asked to use as the basis for answering questions.

4) Observation
A popular test for law-enforcement positions is the observation test. A picture is shown to you for several minutes, then taken away. Questions about the picture test your ability to observe both details and larger elements.

5) Following directions
In many positions in the public service, the employee must be able to carry out written instructions dependably and accurately. You may be given a chart with several columns, each column listing a variety of information. The questions require you to carry out directions involving the information given in the chart.

6) Skills and aptitudes
Performance tests effectively measure some manual skills and aptitudes. When the skill is one in which you are trained, such as typing or shorthand, you can practice. These tests are often very much like those given in business school or high school courses. For many of the other skills and aptitudes, however, no short-time preparation can be made. Skills and abilities natural to you or that you have developed throughout your lifetime are being tested.

Many of the general questions just described provide all the data needed to answer the questions and ask you to use your reasoning ability to find the answers. Your best preparation for these tests, as well as for tests of facts and ideas, is to be at your physical and mental best. You, no doubt, have your own methods of getting into an exam-taking mood and keeping "in shape." The next section lists some ideas on this subject.

IV. KINDS OF QUESTIONS

Only rarely is the "essay" question, which you answer in narrative form, used in civil service tests. Civil service tests are usually of the short-answer type. Full instructions for answering these questions will be given to you at the examination. But in case this is your first experience with short-answer questions and separate answer sheets, here is what you need to know:

1) Multiple-choice Questions
Most popular of the short-answer questions is the "multiple choice" or "best answer" question. It can be used, for example, to test for factual knowledge, ability to solve problems or judgment in meeting situations found at work.
A multiple-choice question is normally one of three types—
- It can begin with an incomplete statement followed by several possible endings. You are to find the one ending which *best* completes the statement, although some of the others may not be entirely wrong.
- It can also be a complete statement in the form of a question which is answered by choosing one of the statements listed.

- It can be in the form of a problem – again you select the best answer.

Here is an example of a multiple-choice question with a discussion which should give you some clues as to the method for choosing the right answer:

When an employee has a complaint about his assignment, the action which will *best* help him overcome his difficulty is to
- A. discuss his difficulty with his coworkers
- B. take the problem to the head of the organization
- C. take the problem to the person who gave him the assignment
- D. say nothing to anyone about his complaint

In answering this question, you should study each of the choices to find which is best. Consider choice "A" – Certainly an employee may discuss his complaint with fellow employees, but no change or improvement can result, and the complaint remains unresolved. Choice "B" is a poor choice since the head of the organization probably does not know what assignment you have been given, and taking your problem to him is known as "going over the head" of the supervisor. The supervisor, or person who made the assignment, is the person who can clarify it or correct any injustice. Choice "C" is, therefore, correct. To say nothing, as in choice "D," is unwise. Supervisors have and interest in knowing the problems employees are facing, and the employee is seeking a solution to his problem.

2) True/False Questions

The "true/false" or "right/wrong" form of question is sometimes used. Here a complete statement is given. Your job is to decide whether the statement is right or wrong.

SAMPLE: A roaming cell-phone call to a nearby city costs less than a non-roaming call to a distant city.

This statement is wrong, or false, since roaming calls are more expensive.

This is not a complete list of all possible question forms, although most of the others are variations of these common types. You will always get complete directions for answering questions. Be sure you understand *how* to mark your answers – ask questions until you do.

V. RECORDING YOUR ANSWERS

Computer terminals are used more and more today for many different kinds of exams.

For an examination with very few applicants, you may be told to record your answers in the test booklet itself. Separate answer sheets are much more common. If this separate answer sheet is to be scored by machine – and this is often the case – it is highly important that you mark your answers correctly in order to get credit.

An electronic scoring machine is often used in civil service offices because of the speed with which papers can be scored. Machine-scored answer sheets must be marked with a pencil, which will be given to you. This pencil has a high graphite content which responds to the electronic scoring machine. As a matter of fact, stray dots may register as answers, so do not let your pencil rest on the answer sheet while you are pondering the correct answer. Also, if your pencil lead breaks or is otherwise defective, ask for another.

Since the answer sheet will be dropped in a slot in the scoring machine, be careful not to bend the corners or get the paper crumpled.

The answer sheet normally has five vertical columns of numbers, with 30 numbers to a column. These numbers correspond to the question numbers in your test booklet. After each number, going across the page are four or five pairs of dotted lines. These short dotted lines have small letters or numbers above them. The first two pairs may also have a "T" or "F" above the letters. This indicates that the first two pairs only are to be used if the questions are of the true-false type. If the questions are multiple choice, disregard the "T" and "F" and pay attention only to the small letters or numbers.

Answer your questions in the manner of the sample that follows:

32. The largest city in the United States is
    A. Washington, D.C.
    B. New York City
    C. Chicago
    D. Detroit
    E. San Francisco

1) Choose the answer you think is best. (New York City is the largest, so "B" is correct.)
2) Find the row of dotted lines numbered the same as the question you are answering. (Find row number 32)
3) Find the pair of dotted lines corresponding to the answer. (Find the pair of lines under the mark "B.")
4) Make a solid black mark between the dotted lines.

VI. BEFORE THE TEST

Common sense will help you find procedures to follow to get ready for an examination. Too many of us, however, overlook these sensible measures. Indeed, nervousness and fatigue have been found to be the most serious reasons why applicants fail to do their best on civil service tests. Here is a list of reminders:

- Begin your preparation early – Don't wait until the last minute to go scurrying around for books and materials or to find out what the position is all about.
- Prepare continuously – An hour a night for a week is better than an all-night cram session. This has been definitely established. What is more, a night a week for a month will return better dividends than crowding your study into a shorter period of time.
- Locate the place of the exam – You have been sent a notice telling you when and where to report for the examination. If the location is in a different town or otherwise unfamiliar to you, it would be well to inquire the best route and learn something about the building.
- Relax the night before the test – Allow your mind to rest. Do not study at all that night. Plan some mild recreation or diversion; then go to bed early and get a good night's sleep.
- Get up early enough to make a leisurely trip to the place for the test – This way unforeseen events, traffic snarls, unfamiliar buildings, etc. will not upset you.
- Dress comfortably – A written test is not a fashion show. You will be known by number and not by name, so wear something comfortable.

- Leave excess paraphernalia at home – Shopping bags and odd bundles will get in your way. You need bring only the items mentioned in the official notice you received; usually everything you need is provided. Do not bring reference books to the exam. They will only confuse those last minutes and be taken away from you when in the test room.
- Arrive somewhat ahead of time – If because of transportation schedules you must get there very early, bring a newspaper or magazine to take your mind off yourself while waiting.
- Locate the examination room – When you have found the proper room, you will be directed to the seat or part of the room where you will sit. Sometimes you are given a sheet of instructions to read while you are waiting. Do not fill out any forms until you are told to do so; just read them and be prepared.
- Relax and prepare to listen to the instructions
- If you have any physical problem that may keep you from doing your best, be sure to tell the test administrator. If you are sick or in poor health, you really cannot do your best on the exam. You can come back and take the test some other time.

VII. AT THE TEST

The day of the test is here and you have the test booklet in your hand. The temptation to get going is very strong. Caution! There is more to success than knowing the right answers. You must know how to identify your papers and understand variations in the type of short-answer question used in this particular examination. Follow these suggestions for maximum results from your efforts:

1) Cooperate with the monitor

The test administrator has a duty to create a situation in which you can be as much at ease as possible. He will give instructions, tell you when to begin, check to see that you are marking your answer sheet correctly, and so on. He is not there to guard you, although he will see that your competitors do not take unfair advantage. He wants to help you do your best.

2) Listen to all instructions

Don't jump the gun! Wait until you understand all directions. In most civil service tests you get more time than you need to answer the questions. So don't be in a hurry. Read each word of instructions until you clearly understand the meaning. Study the examples, listen to all announcements and follow directions. Ask questions if you do not understand what to do.

3) Identify your papers

Civil service exams are usually identified by number only. You will be assigned a number; you must not put your name on your test papers. Be sure to copy your number correctly. Since more than one exam may be given, copy your exact examination title.

4) Plan your time

Unless you are told that a test is a "speed" or "rate of work" test, speed itself is usually not important. Time enough to answer all the questions will be provided, but this does not mean that you have all day. An overall time limit has been set. Divide the total time (in minutes) by the number of questions to determine the approximate time you have for each question.

5) Do not linger over difficult questions

If you come across a difficult question, mark it with a paper clip (useful to have along) and come back to it when you have been through the booklet. One caution if you do this – be sure to skip a number on your answer sheet as well. Check often to be sure that you have not lost your place and that you are marking in the row numbered the same as the question you are answering.

6) Read the questions

Be sure you know what the question asks! Many capable people are unsuccessful because they failed to *read* the questions correctly.

7) Answer all questions

Unless you have been instructed that a penalty will be deducted for incorrect answers, it is better to guess than to omit a question.

8) Speed tests

It is often better NOT to guess on speed tests. It has been found that on timed tests people are tempted to spend the last few seconds before time is called in marking answers at random – without even reading them – in the hope of picking up a few extra points. To discourage this practice, the instructions may warn you that your score will be "corrected" for guessing. That is, a penalty will be applied. The incorrect answers will be deducted from the correct ones, or some other penalty formula will be used.

9) Review your answers

If you finish before time is called, go back to the questions you guessed or omitted to give them further thought. Review other answers if you have time.

10) Return your test materials

If you are ready to leave before others have finished or time is called, take ALL your materials to the monitor and leave quietly. Never take any test material with you. The monitor can discover whose papers are not complete, and taking a test booklet may be grounds for disqualification.

VIII. EXAMINATION TECHNIQUES

1) Read the general instructions carefully. These are usually printed on the first page of the exam booklet. As a rule, these instructions refer to the timing of the examination; the fact that you should not start work until the signal and must stop work at a signal, etc. If there are any *special* instructions, such as a choice of questions to be answered, make sure that you note this instruction carefully.

2) When you are ready to start work on the examination, that is as soon as the signal has been given, read the instructions to each question booklet, underline any key words or phrases, such as *least, best, outline, describe* and the like. In this way you will tend to answer as requested rather than discover on reviewing your paper that you *listed without describing*, that you selected the *worst* choice rather than the *best* choice, etc.

3) If the examination is of the objective or multiple-choice type – that is, each question will also give a series of possible answers: A, B, C or D, and you are called upon to select the best answer and write the letter next to that answer on your answer paper – it is advisable to start answering each question in turn. There may be anywhere from 50 to 100 such questions in the three or four hours allotted and you can see how much time would be taken if you read through all the questions before beginning to answer any. Furthermore, if you come across a question or group of questions which you know would be difficult to answer, it would undoubtedly affect your handling of all the other questions.

4) If the examination is of the essay type and contains but a few questions, it is a moot point as to whether you should read all the questions before starting to answer any one. Of course, if you are given a choice – say five out of seven and the like – then it is essential to read all the questions so you can eliminate the two that are most difficult. If, however, you are asked to answer all the questions, there may be danger in trying to answer the easiest one first because you may find that you will spend too much time on it. The best technique is to answer the first question, then proceed to the second, etc.

5) Time your answers. Before the exam begins, write down the time it started, then add the time allowed for the examination and write down the time it must be completed, then divide the time available somewhat as follows:
    - If 3-1/2 hours are allowed, that would be 210 minutes. If you have 80 objective-type questions, that would be an average of 2-1/2 minutes per question. Allow yourself no more than 2 minutes per question, or a total of 160 minutes, which will permit about 50 minutes to review.
    - If for the time allotment of 210 minutes there are 7 essay questions to answer, that would average about 30 minutes a question. Give yourself only 25 minutes per question so that you have about 35 minutes to review.

6) The most important instruction is to *read each question* and make sure you know what is wanted. The second most important instruction is to *time yourself properly* so that you answer every question. The third most important instruction is to *answer every question*. Guess if you have to but include something for each question. Remember that you will receive no credit for a blank and will probably receive some credit if you write something in answer to an essay question. If you guess a letter – say "B" for a multiple-choice question – you may have guessed right. If you leave a blank as an answer to a multiple-choice question, the examiners may respect your feelings but it will not add a point to your score. Some exams may penalize you for wrong answers, so in such cases *only*, you may not want to guess unless you have some basis for your answer.

7) Suggestions
    a. Objective-type questions
        1. Examine the question booklet for proper sequence of pages and questions
        2. Read all instructions carefully
        3. Skip any question which seems too difficult; return to it after all other questions have been answered
        4. Apportion your time properly; do not spend too much time on any single question or group of questions

5. Note and underline key words – *all, most, fewest, least, best, worst, same, opposite*, etc.
6. Pay particular attention to negatives
7. Note unusual option, e.g., unduly long, short, complex, different or similar in content to the body of the question
8. Observe the use of "hedging" words – *probably, may, most likely*, etc.
9. Make sure that your answer is put next to the same number as the question
10. Do not second-guess unless you have good reason to believe the second answer is definitely more correct
11. Cross out original answer if you decide another answer is more accurate; do not erase until you are ready to hand your paper in
12. Answer all questions; guess unless instructed otherwise
13. Leave time for review

b. Essay questions
1. Read each question carefully
2. Determine exactly what is wanted. Underline key words or phrases.
3. Decide on outline or paragraph answer
4. Include many different points and elements unless asked to develop any one or two points or elements
5. Show impartiality by giving pros and cons unless directed to select one side only
6. Make and write down any assumptions you find necessary to answer the questions
7. Watch your English, grammar, punctuation and choice of words
8. Time your answers; don't crowd material

8) Answering the essay question

Most essay questions can be answered by framing the specific response around several key words or ideas. Here are a few such key words or ideas:

M's: manpower, materials, methods, money, management
P's: purpose, program, policy, plan, procedure, practice, problems, pitfalls, personnel, public relations

a. Six basic steps in handling problems:
1. Preliminary plan and background development
2. Collect information, data and facts
3. Analyze and interpret information, data and facts
4. Analyze and develop solutions as well as make recommendations
5. Prepare report and sell recommendations
6. Install recommendations and follow up effectiveness

b. Pitfalls to avoid
1. *Taking things for granted* – A statement of the situation does not necessarily imply that each of the elements is necessarily true; for example, a complaint may be invalid and biased so that all that can be taken for granted is that a complaint has been registered

2. *Considering only one side of a situation* – Wherever possible, indicate several alternatives and then point out the reasons you selected the best one
3. *Failing to indicate follow up* – Whenever your answer indicates action on your part, make certain that you will take proper follow-up action to see how successful your recommendations, procedures or actions turn out to be
4. *Taking too long in answering any single question* – Remember to time your answers properly

IX. AFTER THE TEST

Scoring procedures differ in detail among civil service jurisdictions although the general principles are the same. Whether the papers are hand-scored or graded by machine we have described, they are nearly always graded by number. That is, the person who marks the paper knows only the number – never the name – of the applicant. Not until all the papers have been graded will they be matched with names. If other tests, such as training and experience or oral interview ratings have been given, scores will be combined. Different parts of the examination usually have different weights. For example, the written test might count 60 percent of the final grade, and a rating of training and experience 40 percent. In many jurisdictions, veterans will have a certain number of points added to their grades.

After the final grade has been determined, the names are placed in grade order and an eligible list is established. There are various methods for resolving ties between those who get the same final grade – probably the most common is to place first the name of the person whose application was received first. Job offers are made from the eligible list in the order the names appear on it. You will be notified of your grade and your rank as soon as all these computations have been made. This will be done as rapidly as possible.

People who are found to meet the requirements in the announcement are called "eligibles." Their names are put on a list of eligible candidates. An eligible's chances of getting a job depend on how high he stands on this list and how fast agencies are filling jobs from the list.

When a job is to be filled from a list of eligibles, the agency asks for the names of people on the list of eligibles for that job. When the civil service commission receives this request, it sends to the agency the names of the three people highest on this list. Or, if the job to be filled has specialized requirements, the office sends the agency the names of the top three persons who meet these requirements from the general list.

The appointing officer makes a choice from among the three people whose names were sent to him. If the selected person accepts the appointment, the names of the others are put back on the list to be considered for future openings.

That is the rule in hiring from all kinds of eligible lists, whether they are for typist, carpenter, chemist, or something else. For every vacancy, the appointing officer has his choice of any one of the top three eligibles on the list. This explains why the person whose name is on top of the list sometimes does not get an appointment when some of the persons lower on the list do. If the appointing officer chooses the second or third eligible, the No. 1 eligible does not get a job at once, but stays on the list until he is appointed or the list is terminated.

X. HOW TO PASS THE INTERVIEW TEST

The examination for which you applied requires an oral interview test. You have already taken the written test and you are now being called for the interview test – the final part of the formal examination.

You may think that it is not possible to prepare for an interview test and that there are no procedures to follow during an interview. Our purpose is to point out some things you can do in advance that will help you and some good rules to follow and pitfalls to avoid while you are being interviewed.

What is an interview supposed to test?

The written examination is designed to test the technical knowledge and competence of the candidate; the oral is designed to evaluate intangible qualities, not readily measured otherwise, and to establish a list showing the relative fitness of each candidate – as measured against his competitors – for the position sought. Scoring is not on the basis of "right" and "wrong," but on a sliding scale of values ranging from "not passable" to "outstanding." As a matter of fact, it is possible to achieve a relatively low score without a single "incorrect" answer because of evident weakness in the qualities being measured.

Occasionally, an examination may consist entirely of an oral test – either an individual or a group oral. In such cases, information is sought concerning the technical knowledges and abilities of the candidate, since there has been no written examination for this purpose. More commonly, however, an oral test is used to supplement a written examination.

Who conducts interviews?

The composition of oral boards varies among different jurisdictions. In nearly all, a representative of the personnel department serves as chairman. One of the members of the board may be a representative of the department in which the candidate would work. In some cases, "outside experts" are used, and, frequently, a businessman or some other representative of the general public is asked to serve. Labor and management or other special groups may be represented. The aim is to secure the services of experts in the appropriate field.

However the board is composed, it is a good idea (and not at all improper or unethical) to ascertain in advance of the interview who the members are and what groups they represent. When you are introduced to them, you will have some idea of their backgrounds and interests, and at least you will not stutter and stammer over their names.

What should be done before the interview?

While knowledge about the board members is useful and takes some of the surprise element out of the interview, there is other preparation which is more substantive. It *is* possible to prepare for an oral interview – in several ways:

1) Keep a copy of your application and review it carefully before the interview

This may be the only document before the oral board, and the starting point of the interview. Know what education and experience you have listed there, and the sequence and dates of all of it. Sometimes the board will ask you to review the highlights of your experience for them; you should not have to hem and haw doing it.

2) Study the class specification and the examination announcement

Usually, the oral board has one or both of these to guide them. The qualities, characteristics or knowledges required by the position sought are stated in these documents. They offer valuable clues as to the nature of the oral interview. For example, if the job involves supervisory responsibilities, the announcement will usually indicate that knowledge of modern supervisory methods and the qualifications of the candidate as a supervisor will be tested. If so, you can expect such questions, frequently in the form of a hypothetical situation which you are expected to solve. NEVER go into an oral without knowledge of the duties and responsibilities of the job you seek.

3) Think through each qualification required

Try to visualize the kind of questions you would ask if you were a board member. How well could you answer them? Try especially to appraise your own knowledge and background in each area, *measured against the job sought*, and identify any areas in which you are weak. Be critical and realistic – do not flatter yourself.

4) Do some general reading in areas in which you feel you may be weak

For example, if the job involves supervision and your past experience has NOT, some general reading in supervisory methods and practices, particularly in the field of human relations, might be useful. Do NOT study agency procedures or detailed manuals. The oral board will be testing your understanding and capacity, not your memory.

5) Get a good night's sleep and watch your general health and mental attitude

You will want a clear head at the interview. Take care of a cold or any other minor ailment, and of course, no hangovers.

What should be done on the day of the interview?

Now comes the day of the interview itself. Give yourself plenty of time to get there. Plan to arrive somewhat ahead of the scheduled time, particularly if your appointment is in the fore part of the day. If a previous candidate fails to appear, the board might be ready for you a bit early. By early afternoon an oral board is almost invariably behind schedule if there are many candidates, and you may have to wait. Take along a book or magazine to read, or your application to review, but leave any extraneous material in the waiting room when you go in for your interview. In any event, relax and compose yourself.

The matter of dress is important. The board is forming impressions about you – from your experience, your manners, your attitude, and your appearance. Give your personal appearance careful attention. Dress your best, but not your flashiest. Choose conservative, appropriate clothing, and be sure it is immaculate. This is a business interview, and your appearance should indicate that you regard it as such. Besides, being well groomed and properly dressed will help boost your confidence.

Sooner or later, someone will call your name and escort you into the interview room. *This is it.* From here on you are on your own. It is too late for any more preparation. But remember, you asked for this opportunity to prove your fitness, and you are here because your request was granted.

What happens when you go in?

The usual sequence of events will be as follows: The clerk (who is often the board stenographer) will introduce you to the chairman of the oral board, who will introduce you to the other members of the board. Acknowledge the introductions before you sit down. Do not be surprised if you find a microphone facing you or a stenotypist sitting by. Oral interviews are usually recorded in the event of an appeal or other review.

Usually the chairman of the board will open the interview by reviewing the highlights of your education and work experience from your application – primarily for the benefit of the other members of the board, as well as to get the material into the record. Do not interrupt or comment unless there is an error or significant misinterpretation; if that is the case, do not hesitate. But do not quibble about insignificant matters. Also, he will usually ask you some question about your education, experience or your present job – partly to get you to start talking and to establish the interviewing "rapport." He may start the actual questioning, or turn it over to one of the other members. Frequently, each member undertakes the questioning on a particular area, one in which he is perhaps most competent, so you can expect each member to participate in the examination. Because time is limited, you may also expect some rather abrupt switches in the direction the questioning takes, so do not be upset by it. Normally, a board member will not pursue a single line of questioning unless he discovers a particular strength or weakness.

After each member has participated, the chairman will usually ask whether any member has any further questions, then will ask you if you have anything you wish to add. Unless you are expecting this question, it may floor you. Worse, it may start you off on an extended, extemporaneous speech. The board is not usually seeking more information. The question is principally to offer you a last opportunity to present further qualifications or to indicate that you have nothing to add. So, if you feel that a significant qualification or characteristic has been overlooked, it is proper to point it out in a sentence or so. Do not compliment the board on the thoroughness of their examination -- they have been sketchy, and you know it. If you wish, merely say, "No thank you, I have nothing further to add." This is a point where you can "talk yourself out" of a good impression or fail to present an important bit of information. Remember, *you close the interview yourself.*

The chairman will then say, "That is all, Mr. _____, thank you." Do not be startled; the interview is over, and quicker than you think. Thank him, gather your belongings and take your leave. Save your sigh of relief for the other side of the door.

How to put your best foot forward

Throughout this entire process, you may feel that the board individually and collectively is trying to pierce your defenses, seek out your hidden weaknesses and embarrass and confuse you. Actually, this is not true. They are obliged to make an appraisal of your qualifications for the job you are seeking, and they want to see you in your best light. Remember, they must interview all candidates and a non-cooperative candidate may become a failure in spite of their best efforts to bring out his qualifications. Here are 15 suggestions that will help you:

1) Be natural – Keep your attitude confident, not cocky

If you are not confident that you can do the job, do not expect the board to be. Do not apologize for your weaknesses, try to bring out your strong points. The board is interested in a positive, not negative, presentation. Cockiness will antagonize any board member and make him wonder if you are covering up a weakness by a false show of strength.

2) Get comfortable, but don't lounge or sprawl

Sit erectly but not stiffly. A careless posture may lead the board to conclude that you are careless in other things, or at least that you are not impressed by the importance of the occasion. Either conclusion is natural, even if incorrect. Do not fuss with your clothing, a pencil or an ashtray. Your hands may occasionally be useful to emphasize a point; do not let them become a point of distraction.

3) Do not wisecrack or make small talk

This is a serious situation, and your attitude should show that you consider it as such. Further, the time of the board is limited -- they do not want to waste it, and neither should you.

4) Do not exaggerate your experience or abilities

In the first place, from information in the application or other interviews and sources, the board may know more about you than you think. Secondly, you probably will not get away with it. An experienced board is rather adept at spotting such a situation, so do not take the chance.

5) If you know a board member, do not make a point of it, yet do not hide it

Certainly you are not fooling him, and probably not the other members of the board. Do not try to take advantage of your acquaintanceship – it will probably do you little good.

6) Do not dominate the interview

Let the board do that. They will give you the clues – do not assume that you have to do all the talking. Realize that the board has a number of questions to ask you, and do not try to take up all the interview time by showing off your extensive knowledge of the answer to the first one.

7) Be attentive

You only have 20 minutes or so, and you should keep your attention at its sharpest throughout. When a member is addressing a problem or question to you, give him your undivided attention. Address your reply principally to him, but do not exclude the other board members.

8) Do not interrupt

A board member may be stating a problem for you to analyze. He will ask you a question when the time comes. Let him state the problem, and wait for the question.

9) Make sure you understand the question

Do not try to answer until you are sure what the question is. If it is not clear, restate it in your own words or ask the board member to clarify it for you. However, do not haggle about minor elements.

10) Reply promptly but not hastily

A common entry on oral board rating sheets is "candidate responded readily," or "candidate hesitated in replies." Respond as promptly and quickly as you can, but do not jump to a hasty, ill-considered answer.

11) Do not be peremptory in your answers

A brief answer is proper – but do not fire your answer back. That is a losing game from your point of view. The board member can probably ask questions much faster than you can answer them.

12) Do not try to create the answer you think the board member wants

He is interested in what kind of mind you have and how it works – not in playing games. Furthermore, he can usually spot this practice and will actually grade you down on it.

13) Do not switch sides in your reply merely to agree with a board member

Frequently, a member will take a contrary position merely to draw you out and to see if you are willing and able to defend your point of view. Do not start a debate, yet do not surrender a good position. If a position is worth taking, it is worth defending.

14) Do not be afraid to admit an error in judgment if you are shown to be wrong

The board knows that you are forced to reply without any opportunity for careful consideration. Your answer may be demonstrably wrong. If so, admit it and get on with the interview.

15) Do not dwell at length on your present job

The opening question may relate to your present assignment. Answer the question but do not go into an extended discussion. You are being examined for a *new* job, not your present one. As a matter of fact, try to phrase ALL your answers in terms of the job for which you are being examined.

Basis of Rating

Probably you will forget most of these "do's" and "don'ts" when you walk into the oral interview room. Even remembering them all will not ensure you a passing grade. Perhaps you did not have the qualifications in the first place. But remembering them will help you to put your best foot forward, without treading on the toes of the board members.

Rumor and popular opinion to the contrary notwithstanding, an oral board wants you to make the best appearance possible. They know you are under pressure – but they also want to see how you respond to it as a guide to what your reaction would be under the pressures of the job you seek. They will be influenced by the degree of poise you display, the personal traits you show and the manner in which you respond.

ABOUT THIS BOOK

This book contains tests divided into Examination Sections. Go through each test, answering every question in the margin. We have also attached a sample answer sheet at the back of the book that can be removed and used. At the end of each test look at the answer key and check your answers. On the ones you got wrong, look at the right answer choice and learn. Do not fill in the answers first. Do not memorize the questions and answers, but understand the answer and principles involved. On your test, the questions will likely be different from the samples. Questions are changed and new ones added. If you understand these past questions you should have success with any changes that arise. Tests may consist of several types of questions. We have additional books on each subject should more study be advisable or necessary for you. Finally, the more you study, the better prepared you will be. This book is intended to be the last thing you study before you walk into the examination room. Prior study of relevant texts is also recommended. NLC publishes some of these in our Fundamental Series. Knowledge and good sense are important factors in passing your exam. Good luck also helps. So now study this Passbook, absorb the material contained within and take that knowledge into the examination. Then do your best to pass that exam.

EXAMINATION SECTION

EXAMINATION SECTION
TEST 1

DIRECTIONS: Each question or incomplete statement is followed by several suggested answers or completions. Select the one that BEST answers the question or completes the statement. *PRINT THE LETTER OF THE CORRECT ANSWER IN THE SPACE AT THE RIGHT.*

1. The Social Security Act (the Act) mandates the establishment of minimum health and safety and CLIA standards that must be met by providers and suppliers participating in which programs?
    A. Medicare
    B. Medicaid
    C. Social Security
    D. Both A and B

    1.____

2. What percentage of all health care expenditures are estimated as annual losses due to health care fraud?
    A. 3 – 10%   B. 23 – 30%   C. 15 – 25%   D. 30 – 40%

    2.____

3. According to the legislation for HIPDB, there should be
    A. privacy protection
    B. regular monthly reports
    C. procedures to manage disputes
    D. all of the above

    3.____

4. Which of the following is NOT a function of the states for CMS under the Social Security Act?
    A. Explaining requirements
    B. Conducting investigations
    C. Training employees
    D. Identifying participants

    4.____

5. If the provider refuses to permit examination, the CMS may take action for
    A. termination   B. suspension   C. arrest   D. delay

    5.____

6. According to Medicare terminology, which of the following is a supplier?
    A. Hospital
    B. Ambulatory surgery center
    C. Home health agency
    D. Nursing home

    6.____

7. The term "alcohol abuse" refers to the use of any alcoholic beverage which impairs the user's
    A. physical health
    B. emotional health
    C. social wellbeing
    D. all of the above

    7.____

8. There are a number of methods for monitoring medical audits, as suggested by Harrison. Which of the following is one such method that is based on the concept of acquiring knowledge from mistakes?
    A. Surveys
    B. Observational studies
    C. Peer review
    D. Case studies

    8.____

9. In every hospital, much significance is given to laboratory and diagnostic services. Which of the following BEST explains the reason for this statement?
   A. They receive patients and brief them about investigations.
   B. They maintain good relations between the hospital and its patients.
   C. They ensure patient satisfaction.
   D. They assist in implementation of the latest technologies.

9.____

10. Net death rate is based on which of the following?
    A. The total deaths per 1,000 patients
    B. The deaths after 24 hours of hospital admission
    C. The total number of deaths due to chronic diseases
    D. None of the above

10.____

11. For hospitals and health care management, many different research models are in use. Which of the following models can be used for management of resources?
    A. Linear programming model
    B. Forecasting model
    C. Sequencing model
    D. Simultaneous programming model

11.____

12. Which of the following actors must be considered when studying the existing hospital facilities while planning a hospital?
    A. Patient's expectations
    B. Patient's perceptions
    C. Healthcare professional's perceptions in existing facilities
    D. Physical conditions of existing facilities

12.____

13. Which of the following is a certificate that an organization or hospital meets the nationally recognized standards?
    A. CPHQ   B. CORE   C. AAAHC   D. AHAM

13.____

14. A data collection will have to be arranged for which of the following patients?
    A. A 50-year-old woman who qualifies for Medicaid disability insurance suffers from diabetes and requires drug monitoring.
    B. A 30-year-old woman who has had a Cesarean procedure recently and now suffers from a wound infection.
    C. A 50-year-old man who qualifies for Medicaid and has been in a car accident.
    D. A 60-year-old man suffering from heart failure.

14.____

15. Which of the following cannot usually be assigned discharge planning responsibilities?
    A. Registered nurses   B. Social workers
    C. Family member   D. All of the above

15.____

16. Discharge planning is not required for outpatients.
    A. True   B. False

16.____

17. The types of institutions participating solely in Medicaid include
    A. unskilled nursing facilities
    B. psychiatric residential treatment facilities
    C. intermediate care facilities for the mentally retarded
    D. all of the above

    17.____

18. In accordance with the statement of deficiencies, an institution is given _____ calendar days, during which it must respond with a plan of correction. Failing this, the state agency certifies noncompliance.
    A. 10   B. 15   C. 20   D. 25

    18.____

19. When Medicaid nursing facilities wish to participate as Medicare skilled nursing facilities, the state must conduct a new survey.
    A. True   B. False

    19.____

20. For a long-term nursing facility, the requirements include provision of licensed nursing 24 hours a day as well as provision of registered nurses for 8 hours a day. Under which of the following conditions can the state grant a waiver of these requirements?
    A. If the facility is able to demonstrate that it has made sincere efforts to fulfill the requirements but has been unable to do so
    B. The facility is located in a rural area
    C. The facility is participating in community development programs
    D. The facility can prove that its patients do not require licensed nursing 24 hours a day

    20.____

21. _____ have been established to provide assistance to the personnel conducting surveys.
    A. Survey protocols   B. Interpretive guidelines
    C. Both A and B   D. None of the above

    21.____

22. The CMS regularly sponsors the "open door forums" with the aim of providing opportunity for dialogue between the CMS and the
    A. skilled and unskilled nursing facilities
    B. stakeholder community at large
    C. certified healthcare professionals
    D. investors

    22.____

23. The first part of the interpretive guidelines include
    A. wordings of the regulation
    B. survey tag number
    C. column part guidance to surveyors
    D. survey procedures

    23.____

24. EMTALA was enacted by Congress in the year _____ as a part of the Consolidated Omnibus Budget Reconciliation Act or COBRA.
    A. 2000   B. 1993   C. 1986   D. 1972

    24.____

25. The Healthcare Quality Improvement Act of 1986 was introduced by Congressman _____ from Oregon. 25.____
 A. Ron Wyden
 B. Jerrold Nadler
 C. Nick Rahall
 D. Pete King

___

KEY (CORRECT ANSWERS)

1.	D	11.	A
2.	A	12.	D
3.	D	13.	C
4.	C	14.	A
5.	A	15.	C
6.	B	16.	A
7.	D	17.	D
8.	C	18.	A
9.	A	19.	B
10.	B	20.	A

21.	C
22.	B
23.	B
24.	C
25.	A

TEST 2

DIRECTIONS: Each question or incomplete statement is followed by several suggested answers or completions. Select the one that BEST answers the question or completes the statement. *PRINT THE LETTER OF THE CORRECT ANSWER IN THE SPACE AT THE RIGHT.*

1. Which of the following is an "administrative" aspect of what AAAHC looks for when surveying any organization?
    A. Are the policies in use appropriate for all?
    B. Is the information provided by clients safe?
    C. Are patient satisfaction surveys organized in a timely and efficient manner?
    D. All of the above

    1._____

2. Which of the following is NOT a part of the hospital discharge planning process for patients?
    A. Implementing a complete evaluation process
    B. Maintaining files of facilities where the patient may be transferred
    C. Identifying high risk criteria
    D. Managing the hospital resources

    2._____

3. Medicaid required that the nursing facilities meet the same requirements as the
    A. unskilled nursing facilities
    B. unskilled nursing facilities participating in Medicare
    C. skilled nursing facilities
    D. skilled nursing facilities participating in Medicare

    3._____

4. Under the agreements between the State and the Secretary, the state survey agencies are allowed to enforce the standards for
    A. CLIA   B. Medicaid
    C. CLIA and Medicaid D. none of the above

    4._____

5. A _____ nursing facility has in effect a transfer agreement which meets the requirements of Sections 1861(1), 1866, and 1819 of the Act.
    A. skilled   B. unskilled   C. temporary   D. primary

    5._____

6. Interpretive guidelines have been established to provide guidance to the individuals conducting surveys. These interpretive guidelines include _____ parts.
    A. 2   B. 3   C. 5   D. 7

    6._____

7. The concerns of which of the following are addressed by low-income health access open door forum?
    A. Beneficiary advocates   B. Providers
    C. Information intermediaries   D. All of the above

    7._____

5

8. _____ is also known as COBRA or the patient anti-dumping law.
   A. URAC   B. EMTALA   C. HFAP   D. AAAHC

9. _____ is a nationally recognized accreditation organization which meets or exceeds the CMS standards to provide accreditation to hospitals and other healthcare centers.
   A. HFAP   B. NCQA   C. AAHEA   D. SACS

10. The Joint Commission accredits more than _____ healthcare organizations in the U.S.
    A. 5,000   B. 10,000   C. 20,000   D. 50,000

11. The MOST stringent form of health care regulation is
    A. certification
    B. registering
    C. authorization
    D. licensure

12. Clinical guidelines
    A. are unrelated with the admission process
    B. are formatted in accordance with every guideline approved
    C. consider the continuous provision of care as an important part of patient safety
    D. are specific for every patient

13. Medication _____ refers to the situation when clinical care is not executed properly and a wrong drug is administered or the drug is administered in an incorrect way.
    A. overdose
    B. underuse
    C. irresponsibility
    D. error

14. To which of the following organizations is the CVO certification available?
    A. Organizations that are conducting credentials verification
    B. Organizations which report credentialing information to clients
    C. Organizations which maintain confidentiality of information
    D. All of the above

15. The certification level(s) that a Credentials Verification Organization can achieve include
    A. certification
    B. denial of certification
    C. both A and B
    D. none of the above

16. Which of the following is the United States of America's oldest accreditation organization?
    A. The Joint Commission on Accreditation of Healthcare Organization
    B. The Accreditation Association for Ambulatory Health Care
    C. Medicare
    D. Medicaid

17. The life expectancy of a terminally ill patient is
    A. one month or less
    B. six months or less
    C. one year or less
    D. only a few years

    17._____

18. In the year _____, President Obama's healthcare reforms, known as the "Patient Protection" and the "Affordable Care Act" became a law.
    A. 1999   B. 2000   C. 2005   D. 2010

    18._____

19. Traditionally in the U.S., health insurance has been seen to be less common among young adults. This includes all males and females between the ages of 20 and 29. The reason(s) for this may include the lack of
    A. awareness in this age group
    B. opportunities available to this age group
    C. media involvement in the issue
    D. all of the above

    19._____

20. The target year for complete conversion to Electronic Health Records systems was set by President Obama as _____, following which organizations that fail to undergo this transition shall face payment penalties.
    A. 2014   B. 2016   C. 2020   D. 2024

    20._____

21. The concept of population based healthcare quality is mainly based on
    A. evidence-based research
    B. public relations
    C. measurement of community's health status
    D. achievement of higher patient satisfaction

    21._____

22. According to the URAC policies, what is a measurement year?
    A. The first calendar year following the year in which an organization receives URAC accreditation
    B. The last calendar year before the organization receives URAC accreditation
    C. The year following the reporting year
    D. None of the above

    22._____

23. The three levels of management are
    A. strategic, tactical, and operational
    B. top level, middle level, and first line management
    C. both A and B
    D. none of the above

    23._____

24. The primary healthcare is _____ for the community, as compared to other levels of healthcare.
    A. less expensive
    B. more expensive
    C. less efficient
    D. more efficient

    24._____

25. It is the _____ job to manage procedural changes which are related to safety of patients in the hospital.
    A. first line manager's
    B. top management's
    C. middle management's
    D. every manager's

KEY (CORRECT ANSWERS)

1. A
2. D
3. D
4. C
5. A

6. B
7. D
8. B
9. A
10. C

11. D
12. C
13. D
14. D
15. C

16. A
17. B
18. D
19. D
20. B

21. C
22. A
23. C
24. A
25. D

TEST 3

DIRECTIONS: Each question or incomplete statement is followed by several suggested answers or completions. Select the one that BEST answers the question or completes the statement. *PRINT THE LETTER OF THE CORRECT ANSWER IN THE SPACE AT THE RIGHT.*

1. The accreditation credentialing standards can be traced back to the 1970's with the _____ program. 1.____
    A. Joint Commission Hospital Accreditation
    B. Accreditation Association for Ambulatory Health Care
    C. American Association for Laboratory Accreditation
    D. National Home School Accreditation of America

2. Which of the following is a common requirement to obtain certification? 2.____
    A. Submitting application
    B. Giving an oral exam
    C. Undergoing an ethics examination
    D. All of the above

3. Which of the following is a reason that BEST demonstrates the importance of accreditation? 3.____
    A. It allows professionals to pursue a better career.
    B. It helps the management avoid any obstacles in serving their client.
    C. It shows the values the clients attach to provide services of the state of the art standards.
    D. To attract more investors and build the reputation of the institute.

4. The Joint Commission requires the verification of licensure at four different instances. Three of these include the stage of initial granting, the renewal, and the revision of privileges. Which is the fourth one? 4.____
    A. When mismanagement is experienced
    B. During a crisis situation
    C. If the organization intends to make administration changes
    D. At the time of license expiration

5. Which of the following options shows the CORRECT sequence of events in processing of applications by the Joint Commission? If the provider refuses to permit examination, the CMS may take action for 5.____
    A. receiving application; verifying contents; processing; review by chief; notifying applicant; approval; review and recommendations to the board of trustees
    B. verifying contents; receiving application; review by chief; processing; notifying; approval; review and recommendations to the board of trustees
    C. receive application; verifying contents; processing; review by chief; review and recommendations to the board of trustees; approval; notifying applicant
    D. none of the above

6. In what way is the credentialing process of HFAP different from that of the Joint Commission?
   A. A credential committee may be involved in the process if it exists
   B. It is a more convenient process
   C. No verification of particulars is involved
   D. The chief/chair cannot make recommendations

7. Privileging is different from credentialing as the former involves
   A. the authority given to a clinician
   B. the process a clinician is involved in to gain authority
   C. the attainment of employment
   D. all of the above

8. By applying for the credentialing process, the applicant demonstrates his _____ to appear for interviews regarding the application or credentialing process.
   A. need
   B. excuse
   C. willingness
   D. non-availability

9. The document a candidate may have to provide for primary source verification may include a photocopy of
   A. medical school diploma
   B. birth certificate
   C. training completion certificate
   D. all of the above

10. A self-designation is designed to accommodate those applications who wish to establish their core credentials but have not yet
    A. chosen an entity to receive their profile
    B. completed their qualifications
    C. completed the application
    D. none of the above

11. Every state licensing authority will not have its own application for licensure.
    A. True
    B. False

12. To verify a physician's medical license, the primary source verifiers will check with the physician licensing board in their
    A. area
    B. hospital
    C. state
    D. database

13. The Association of American Medical Colleges, Federation of State Medical Boards and American Academy of Physician Assistants are some of the internet resources available for verification of
    A. application
    B. credentials
    C. hospitals
    D. physicians

14. For the verification of an MD's board certification, the ABMS certified doctor verification program is an unacceptable source because it is
    A. solely intended for consumer reference
    B. not an acceptable verification process
    C. not an authentic verification process
    D. a time-consuming option

15. According to the Joint Commission, the hospital must query the National Practitioner Data Bank at three times. Which of the following is NOT included in these three instances?
    A. Initial granting of privileges
    B. Renewal of privileges
    C. Requesting withdrawal of privileges
    D. Requesting new privileges

15.____

16. A physician's self-query to the NPDB is sufficient to fulfill the Joint Commission's requirements.
    A. True
    B. False

16.____

17. According to the NCQA, an organization can verify the sanctions on licensure in any state where the practitioner
    A. holds a license
    B. ever held a license
    C. provides care
    D. all of the above

17.____

18. The organization with which NCQA allows verification to be done includes FSMB, NPDB, and
    A. ABDB   B. AAAHC   C. HIPDB   D. AMA

18.____

19. Jill works in a small practice and for some modalities she has problems meeting the continuing experience through primary interpretation. Another way to meet the requirement for her is by
    A. an alternative peer review program
    B. an alternative job
    C. reject the option of double-reading
    D. seek another board's assistance

19.____

20. According to the Joint Commission, the information which must be included in peer recommendation includes medical knowledge, professionalism, skills, and
    A. clinical judgment
    B. failures
    C. financial details
    D. educational qualifications

20.____

21. Ongoing monitoring of sanctions to Medicare and Medicaid must be done on a monthly basis or within _____ days.
    A. 15   B. 30   C. 35   D. 40

21.____

22. A credential which must be tracked on an ongoing basis due to the need to keep it current is
    A. security clearance
    B. diplomas
    C. state licensure
    D. identification documents

22.____

23. The NCQA uses the date of _____ as the official date of the application.
    A. retrieval of data
    B. stamping the document as "received"
    C. date on the letter or report
    D. the receipt date

23.____

24. The Joint Commission states that the _____ can grant temporary privileges 24.____
    A. CEO   B. Committee   C. Trustees   D. Manager

25. The Federation of State Medical Boards is an acceptable source for _____ source verification for sanction activity against physicians. 25.____
    A. primary   B. secondary   C. temporary   D. short term

KEY (CORRECT ANSWERS)

1.	A	11.	B
2.	D	12.	C
3.	C	13.	B
4.	D	14.	A
5.	C	15.	C
6.	A	16.	B
7.	A	17.	C
8.	C	18.	C
9.	D	19.	A
10.	A	20.	A

21.	B
22.	C
23.	C
24.	C
25.	A

TEST 4

DIRECTIONS: Each question or incomplete statement is followed by several suggested answers or completions. Select the one that BEST answers the question or completes the statement. *PRINT THE LETTER OF THE CORRECT ANSWER IN THE SPACE AT THE RIGHT.*

1. A motivating benefit of board certification for applicants is   1.____
   A. reduced cost to practice
   B. enhanced salary
   C. demonstrate the value attached to national standards
   D. all of the above

2. A medical staff services association was established by Cochrane and Covell Carpenter in California in the year 1971 and this evolved into a national organization in 1976. This organization is known as _____ and provides education and other resources to its members.   2.____
   A. HFAP   B. NAMSS   C. NCQA   D. URAC

3. The _____ examination has been created particularly for practitioner credentialing in the arena of managed care.   3.____
   A. ECFMG   B. USMLE
   C. CPCS   D. none of the above

4. The difference between a DO and MD is the   4.____
   A. DO is a licensed physician unlike the MD
   B. MD is a licensed physician unlike the DO
   C. DO is an osteopathic physician while an MD is a medical doctor
   D. MD is an osteopathic physician while a DO is a medical doctor

5. The U.S. Congress passed in 1984 the National Organ Transplant Act, according to which the transplantation network is operated by a non-profit organization which is under the _____ contract.   5.____
   A. regional   B. state   C. federal   D. national

6. The _____ is based in Richmond and administers the Organ Procurement and Transplantation Network under contract with the HRSA.   6.____
   A. National Institute of Health
   B. Advisory Committee on Organ Transplantation
   C. U.S. Department of Health and Human Services
   D. United Network for Organ Sharing

7. _____ allows the patient to communicate his preferences in terms of health care in case he becomes unable to make his own decisions.   7.____
   A. Advanced Directive   B. Habitats Directive
   C. Death Directive   D. None of the above

8. A _____ year period for certification has been established by the Commission on Certification. 8.____
   A. 3 B. 5 C. 7 D. 8

9. Primary source verification can be done electronically by mail, fax, or telephone in certain circumstances. 9.____
   A. True B. False

10. A document which an applicant provides directly, rather than by primary or secondary source, is 10.____
    A. acceptable
    B. non-acceptable
    C. acceptable under special circumstances
    D. acceptable if a third party is involved

11. The American Academy of Nurse Practitioners currently charges $40 for verification of national certification. The charge for verification provided to State Boards of Nursing is 11.____
    A. $40 B. $50 C. $75 D. free of cost

12. According to Section 1921 of the Social Security Act, the state must provide the _____ or his designated member with access to documents of authority. 12.____
    A. applicant B. secretary C. CEO D. trustee

13. In accordance with the 1996 Amendments in the electronic Freedom of Information Act, a publicly accessible _____ has to be established by the HRSA. 13.____
    A. website
    B. public reading room
    C. electronic reading room
    D. database

14. The Freedom of Information Act places requesters in three categories for fee purposes. Which of the following is NOT included in these three categories? 14.____
    A. Educational institute or media
    B. Commercial use requesters
    C. Scientific institutes
    D. None of the above

15. About 120 million Americans, or 70% of the total health plan members are covered by _____ health plans. 15.____
    A. NCQA B. AAAHC C. EMTALA D. NPDB

16. The _____ survey is for the new plans to NCQA and leads to a 3-year accreditation. 16.____
    A. first B. second C. interim D. renewal

17. NCQA standards involve a number of categories including Utilization Management. One example of Utilization Management is 17.____
    A. specific plan programs for people with chronic illness
    B. how plan distributes information to members
    C. does the plan use evidence-based guidelines in decision making
    D. all of the above

18. According to the Affordable Care Act, qualified health plans should participate in _____ to report on quality measures.
    A. exchanges   B. discussions   C. keeps   D. investments

19. HFAP has adopted the _____ safe practices which were provided in 2009 by the National Quality Forum.
    A. 31   B. 32   C. 33   D. 34

20. The members of HFAP survey team include three surveyors: a physician, a nurse, and a
    A. clinician
    B. finance manager
    C. hospital administrator
    D. technical assistant

21. According to the National Practitioner Data Bank's report for years 2002 - 2012, the total medical malpractice payments in the United States are around
    A. $150,000   B. $100,000   C. $250,000   D. $400,000

22. The difference between Laboratory Developed Tests and FDA's authority is the premarket clearance and approval method of
    A. FDA to assess the validity of a system in greater depth
    B. LDA to assess the validity of a system in greater depth
    C. FDA to assess the validity of a system in greater scope
    D. none of the above

23. The _____ regional office has the responsibility for approval and certification that ensures that the Regional Nonmedical Health Care Institution meets all conditions of coverage and participation.
    A. California   B. Boston   C. Alaska   D. Kansas

24. According to CMS, which of the following is not a type of organ transplant program?
    A. Heart   B. Lung   C. Brain   D. Pancreas

25. Individuals practicing outside the U.S. are exempt from having to enroll in a peer review program.
    A. True
    B. False
    C. True, until the time they come back to the U.S.
    D. False, until the time they come back to the U.S.

KEY (CORRECT ANSWERS)

1. D
2. B
3. C
4. C
5. C

6. D
7. A
8. B
9. A
10. B

11. D
12. B
13. C
14. D
15. A

16. A
17. C
18. A
19. D
20. C

21. A
22. A
23. B
24. C
25. C

EXAMINATION SECTION
TEST 1

DIRECTIONS: Each question or incomplete statement is followed by several suggested answers or completions. Select the one that BEST answers the question or completes the statement. *PRINT THE LETTER OF THE CORRECT ANSWER IN THE SPACE AT THE RIGHT.*

1. The AAAHC has organized a number of clinical studies on the cataract and lens operations since 1999. The procedure usually involved adults over the age of
    A. 30   B. 40   C. 50   D. 60

    1.____

2. Almost _____% of colonoscopies, particularly those for detecting colorectal cancer, are conducted in an ambulatory setting.
    A. 30   B. 45   C. 60   D. unknown

    2.____

3. Accreditation may be described as a "voluntary" regulatory requirement.
    A. True
    B. False
    C. True, except in some cases
    D. False, except in some cases

    3.____

4. Which of the following is a major accrediting organization for hospitals and surgery centers?
    A. AAAHC
    B. AAAASF
    C. JCAHO
    D. All of the above

    4.____

5. Which of the following explains the benefit of accreditation?
    A. It increases efficiency.
    B. It reduces cost.
    C. It helps motivate staff members.
    D. All of the above

    5.____

6. When was the AAAHC formed?
    A. 1969   B. 1979   C. 1989   D. 1999

    6.____

7. The term "ambulatory" in AAAHC covers which of the following?
    A. Ambulatory surgery centers
    B. Community health centers
    C. HMO's
    D. All of the above

    7.____

8. Organizations which apply at AAAHC may receive any one of the _____ total rankings.
    A. three   B. five   C. seven   D. nine

    8.____

17

9. The _____ rank at AAAHC shows that the facility does not meet the standards currently but is allowed to re-apply after a period of 6 months has elapsed.
   A. 6 month accreditation   B. Denial
   C. Deferred   D. None of the above

10. The AAAASF accredits _____ which are owned or operated by the American Board of Medical Specialties.
    A. single specialty   B. multi-specialty
    C. both A and B   D. none of the above

11. For the purpose of accreditation, the facilities must be _____ compliant with an organization's set of standards.
    A. 100%   B. 90%   C. 80%   D. 50%

12. The accreditation program at AAAASF addresses a total of _____ aspects of the outpatient surgery center.
    A. three   B. five   C. seven D. nine

13. Costs of accreditation depends on
    A. the sized of the facility applying for accreditation
    B. the number of specialties
    C. both A and B
    D. none of the above

14. The Joint Commission grants one of the total _____ accreditation levels to its applicants.
    A. three   B. six   C. nine   D. ten

15. Medicaid and CHIP cover more than _____ million children.
    A. 81   B. 55   C. 31   D. 11

16. Medicare Part A covers which of the following?
    A. X-rays   B. Hospitalization cost
    C. Prescription drugs   D. All of the above

17. Medicare Part C covers which of the following?
    A. Hospitalization costs   B. Medicare Advantage Plan
    C. Prescription drugs   D. All of the above

18. The monthly income limit is $993 for individuals and $1331 for couples in all states except Alaska and
    A. Hawaii   B. Ohio   C. New York   D. New Jersey

19. A national minimum eligibility standard of _____ has been created by the ACA for the federal poverty level.
    A. 65%   B. 88%   C. 100%   D. 133%

20. _____ is included in eligibility groups for Medicaid.
    A. Medically needed
    B. Breast cancer prevention
    C. TB patients
    D. All of the above

21. Operating Department Practitioners work with
    A. surgeons
    B. nurses
    C. anesthetists
    D. all of the above

22. HFAP was conceived in 1943 and began surveying hospitals in the year
    A. 1945   B. 1948   C. 1953   D. 1966

23. "Clinical Invasive Ventilation" refers to standards offered by
    A. HFAP   B. HQAA   C. AAAHC   D. AARC

24. Section 302 of the Medicare Modernization Act requires the formation of new competitive bidding programs for which of the following?
    A. Oncologists
    B. Dentists
    C. Prosthetics
    D. None of the above

25. Medtronic has recently decided to buy Covidien on a value of approximately _____ billion.
    A. 10   B. 20   C. 30   D. 40

KEY (CORRECT ANSWERS)

1.	B	11.	A
2.	C	12.	D
3.	A	13.	C
4.	D	14.	B
5.	D	15.	C
6.	B	16.	B
7.	D	17.	B
8.	B	18.	A
9.	C	19.	D
10.	C	20.	D

21. D
22. A
23. B
24. C
25. D

TEST 2

DIRECTIONS: Each question or incomplete statement is followed by several suggested answers or completions. Select the one that BEST answers the question or completes the statement. *PRINT THE LETTER OF THE CORRECT ANSWER IN THE SPACE AT THE RIGHT.*

1. _____ at the Joint Commission shows the decision that there exists justification to deny accreditation as it failed to show satisfactory compliance but the decision is subject to review.
    A. Preliminary denial
    B. Accreditation denial
    C. Conditional accreditation
    D. Provisional accreditation

   1.____

2. When a facility meets only a subset of standards during the preliminary evaluation and it must undergo a full survey after 6 months, it is termed _____ by the Joint Commission.
    A. Preliminary denial
    B. Accreditation denial
    C. Conditional accreditation
    D. Provisional accreditation

   2.____

3. _____ accreditation at the Joint Commission signifies that an organization has failed to demonstrate its compliance in multiple areas and it must achieve compliance within a given time.
    A. Conditional
    B. Provisional
    C. Preliminary denial
    D. Accreditation denial

   3.____

4. JCAHO has been accrediting ambulatory surgical centers since
    A. 1945   B. 1955   C. 1965   D. 1975

   4.____

5. About 50% of the JCAHO standards are linked with
    A. safety
    B. environment
    C. punctuality
    D. medication use

   5.____

6. _____ is recognized by Medicare and has a deemed status.
    A. JCAHO
    B. AAAHC
    C. AAAASF
    D. All of the above

   6.____

7. _____ accreditation is originally referred to as a deemed status.
    A. AAAHC
    B. Medicare
    C. JC
    D. None of the above

   7.____

8. The survey process for a Medicare survey depends on the chosen AO.
    A. True
    B. False

   8.____

9. When are Medicare surveys announced?
    A. One week before the survey
    B. One month before the survey
    C. Six months before the survey
    D. None of the above

   9.____

10. The survey period for Medicare survey is a _____ day span.
    A. 14   B. 30   C. 60   D. 90

    10.____

11. It is expected by Medicare that the ASC shall provide information to patients at least _____ day(s) ahead of the scheduled procedure, about the ASC's ownership interests and information about patient rights or advanced directives.
    A. 1 B. 2 C. 3 D. 4

12. A unique aspect of the Medicare accreditation process is that once a survey is completed, the ASC is presented with a statement of _____, which details its findings.
    A. findings
    B. deficiencies
    C. compliance
    D. accreditation

13. The governing body of any ASC can establish its own minimum qualifications, as in terms of education, based on the national standards and _____ requirements.
    A. state B. regional C. international D. federal

14. Title 18 of the Social Security Amendments established Medicare for Americans over the age of
    A. 45 B. 55 C. 65 D. 75

15. The Physician Quality Reporting System provides incentive payment to practices identified with
    A. national provider identifier
    B. tax identification number
    C. both A and B
    D. none of the above

16. _____ refers to the prescriber's ability of electronically sending prescriptions to the pharmacy from his point of care.
    A. E-health
    B. Telemarketing
    C. E-prescribing
    D. None of the above

17. _____ may be described as the use of web services for health care.
    A. E-health
    B. Telemarketing
    C. E-prescribing
    D. None of the above

18. A difference between Medicare and Medicaid HER incentive program is
    A. Medicare program is run by CMS while Medicaid is run by the State Medicaid Agency
    B. Medicare program is run by the State Medicaid Agency while Medicaid is run by CMS
    C. Both are run by CMS
    D. Both are run by the State Medicaid Agency

19. Medicaid HER incentive program involves payments over _____ years which do not have to be consecutive.
    A. three B. four C. five D. six

20. Which of the following BEST describes URAC?
    A. For profit
    B. Non-profit
    C. Governmental
    D. All of the above

21. According to a recent report by the CDC, approximately _____ of the U.S. population suffers from diabetes.\
    A. 5%   B. 9%   C. 17%   D. 55%

22. This year the Joint Commission International is celebrating _____ years of global impact on health care.
    A. 10   B. 20   C. 30   D. 40

23. The total number of registered hospitals in the U.S. is approximately
    A. 6,000   B. 4,000   C. 3,000   D. 8,000

24. _____ is a way of preventing mistakes when serving clients or customers.
    A. Quality assurance   B. Risk management
    C. Risk avoidance   D. Functional assessment

25. According to a new CMS proposal, Medicare shall make reasonable effort to render a decision on prior authorization requests within _____ days.
    A. five   B. ten   C. fifteen   D. twenty

KEY (CORRECT ANSWERS)

1.	A	11.	A
2.	D	12.	B
3.	C	13.	A
4.	D	14.	C
5.	A	15.	C
6.	D	16.	C
7.	B	17.	A
8.	B	18.	B
9.	D	19.	D
10.	D	20.	B

21.	B
22.	B
23.	A
24.	A
25.	B

TEST 3

DIRECTIONS: Each question or incomplete statement is followed by several suggested answers or completions. Select the one that BEST answers the question or completes the statement. *PRINT THE LETTER OF THE CORRECT ANSWER IN THE SPACE AT THE RIGHT.*

1. Medicare and Medicaid were direct outgrowths of _____ program.
   A. Kerr-Mills
   B. Beer-Mills
   C. Herr-Mills
   D. none of the above

   1.____

2. Between 2011 and 2012, teen birth rates have decreased by approximately
   A. 5%   B. 35%   C. 45%   D. 75%

   2.____

3. In October 2006, Jay Schindler won his case when the defendant's motion for summary judgment under HCQIA was
   A. accepted
   B. denied
   C. postponed
   D. none of the above

   3.____

4. _____ is the process through which a professional review body considers whether a practitioner's membership will be negatively impacted by his competence or conduct.
   A. Credentialing
   B. Privileging
   C. Peer review
   D. None of the above

   4.____

5. The National Practitioner Data Bank was actually promulgated by the _____ of 1986.
   A. AAAHC
   B. JC
   C. HCQIA
   D. all of the above

   5.____

6. The information on the NPDB is available to which of the following?
   A. General public
   B. Practitioners
   C. Patients
   D. None of the above

   6.____

7. It was reported by almost _____ of hospitals in the Leapfrog survey of 2008 that they had adopted a no bill policy for adverse events.
   A. 60%   B. 40%   C. 30%   D. 7%

   7.____

8. According to the NPDB research statistics, the population of America in 2013 was approximately
   A. 250,000,000   B. 320,000,000   C. 300,000,000   D. 200,000,000

   8.____

9. In the year 2012, NPDB expanded its website to provide statistical data of _____ years in tabular and graphical form.
   A. 10   B. 20   C. 30   D. 40

   9.____

10. According to the Title IV of Public Law 99-660, there has been a _____ occurrence of medical malpractice.
    A. decreasing   B. stabilizing   C. increasing   D. varying

    10.____

11. HCQIA required the reporters of NPDB submit any information related to malpractice payments which were taken on or after the year
    A. 1990   B. 1995   C. 2000   D. 2005

12. Under the Nurse Licensure Compact, the _____ was developed to allow any reporting of the actions against the privilege to practice for a nurse.
    A. Nurse Multi-State Privilege Adverse Action Classification Codes
    B. Nurse Multi-State Credentialing Adverse Action Classification Codes
    C. Nurse Multi-State Negative Action Reporting Codes

13. A payment made at which of the following cannot be reported?
    A. Low end payment
    B. Low end payment under high-low agreement
    C. Low end payment under high agreement
    D. High end payment

14. The denial of the licensure renewal of any physician cannot be reported to the NPDB.
    A. True
    B. False

15. URAC is the acronym for _____ Accreditation Commission.
    A. Uniform Review
    B. Utilization Review
    C. Utilization Research
    D. none of the above

16. Credentialing can be helpful for an organization by
    A. setting standards
    B. maintaining quality of care
    C. both A and B
    D. none of the above

17. The inclusion of PA's in the credentialing process is important for maintaining quality of care and its costs.
    A. True
    B. False
    C. True for U.S. residents only
    D. True for Canadian residents only

18. The term _____ is used to describe populations according their size, structure, and distribution.
    A. census
    B. demographics
    C. geography
    D. behaviorgraphics

19. The "Doorway Thoughts" is a tool which provides general considerations for _____ groups to facilitate conversations between clinicians and older adults.
    A. social
    B. gender-based
    C. ethnic
    D. racial

20. URAC is currently run by over _____ committee volunteers and paid staff.
    A. 100   B. 200   C. 300   D. 500

21. Which of the following is an appropriate credentialing organization for radiologists?
    A. AAAHC   B. SRRT   C. MRRT   D. ARRT

22. Credentialing is based on
    A. costs paid
    B. objectivity
    C. personal bias
    D. none of the above

23. _____ is established by law and is implemented at a state level.
    A. Credentialing
    B. Privileging
    C. Licensure
    D. None of the above

24. Which of the following is an example of primary care setting?
    A. Treatment of severe burns
    B. Physical therapists
    C. Treatment of diabetes
    D. All of the above

25. Which of the following is an example of tertiary care setting?
    A. Depression treatment
    B. Nutritionists
    C. Speech therapists
    D. Neurosurgery

KEY (CORRECT ANSWERS)

1.	B	11.	A
2.	A	12.	A
3.	B	13.	B
4.	C	14.	B
5.	C	15.	B
6.	D	16.	C
7.	A	17.	A
8.	C	18.	B
9.	A	19.	C
10.	C	20.	D

21. D
22. B
23. C
24. C
25. D

TEST 4

DIRECTIONS: Each question or incomplete statement is followed by several suggested answers or completions. Select the one that BEST answers the question or completes the statement. *PRINT THE LETTER OF THE CORRECT ANSWER IN THE SPACE AT THE RIGHT.*

1. In 2014 the Secretary for Health and Human Services is
   A. Sylvia Burwell
   B. Sylvia Goodwell
   C. Andy Slavitt
   D. Andy Burwell

   1.____

2. In 2014, CMS announced that it shall fill two new leaders, a permanent marketplace CEO and a new permanent marketplace
   A. RO
   B. MD
   C. CTO
   D. none of the above

   2.____

3. The most popular plan type in the marketplace, according to HHS, is the _____ plan.
   A. gold
   B. premium
   C. silver
   D. none of the above

   3.____

4. On an average, consumers can select from a total of five health insurers and _____ marketplace plans.
   A. 35   B. 47   C. 55   D. 76

   4.____

5. In the year 2012, about _____ consumers got refunds amounting to half a billion dollars.
   A. 10,000   B. 8.5 million   C. 10 million   D. 30 million

   5.____

6. Which of the following refers to the Healthcare Quality Improvement Act of 1986?
   Title _____ of the United States Code
   A. 101   B. 42   C. 31   D. 11

   6.____

7. The Omnibus Budget Reconciliation Act of _____ introduced the requirement of state medical boards reporting any negative action or finding.
   A. 1958   B. 1965   C. 1991   D. 2000

   7.____

8. EMTALA was originally known as a _____ advisory group
   A. technical
   B. medical
   C. Medicaid
   D. none of the above

   8.____

9. According to Section 945 of the MMA, EMTALA was to be composed of _____ members.
   A. 10   B. 15   C. 19   D. 20

   9.____

2 (#4)

10. Which of the following is the first touch point for those suspecting Medicaid fraud?
    A. Federal Medicaid Agency
    B. State Medicaid Agency
    C. National Medicaid Agency
    D. International Healthcare Agencies

    10._____

11. When reporting fraud, the pertinent information must include which of the following?
    A. Medicaid card number of client
    B. Date of service
    C. Amount of money paid
    D. All of the above

    11._____

12. The beneficiary card sharing tool kit is related to the issues associated with _____ cards.
    A. Medicare
    B. Medicaid
    C. both A and B
    D. none of the above

    12._____

13. _____ care involves highly specialized equipment and expertise.
    A. Primary
    B. Secondary
    C. Tertiary
    D. All of the above

    13._____

14. When distance medicine is facilitated with the use of computers and internet, it is termed
    A. portability
    B. tele health
    c. telemarketing
    D. cyber medicine

    14._____

15. The process of attestation at the data bank allows the accounting for professionals not included in the _____ most queried professions.
    A. 5   B. 10   C. 12   D. 15

    15._____

16. An organization may have more than one DBID.
    A. True
    B. False
    C. True in the case of organizations with multiple departments
    D. False in the case of organizations with multiple departments

    16._____

17. Which of the following cannot query the NPDB at any time?
    A. Medical Malpractice Payers
    B. Health Care Practitioners
    C. State Medical Boards
    D. State Dental Boards

    17._____

18. Hospitals are discouraged to query the data bank more than once every _____ years about a continuous staff practitioner.
    A. 2   B. 3   C. 4   D. 5

    18._____

19. The HIPDB cannot accept reports with dates of action before which of the following?
    A. 1956   B. 1988   C. 1996   D. 2001

    19._____

20. The term "health plan" may include which of the following?
    A. Medicare
    B. U.S. Department of Defense
    C. U.S. Department of Veterans Affairs
    D. All of the above

    20.____

21. If an organization wants to request its members to act as observers during the survey process, according to JC regulations, it must obtain written consent at least _____ days before the survey.
    A. 5   B. 10   C. 15   D. 20

    21.____

22. Internet-based PECO's can be used for which of the following purposes?
    A. Submitting initial Medicare enrollment application
    B. Tracking your application
    C. Withdrawing from the Medicare program
    D. All of the above

    22.____

23. "The conscientious, explicit, and judicious use of current best evidence in making decisions about the care of individual patients." This is the definition for which of the following?
    A. Peer review   B. Evidence-based medicine
    C. Credentialing   D. Privileging

    23.____

24. The current Medicare application fee is
    A. $155   B. $250   C. $532   D. $782

    24.____

25. In November 2006, CMS approved _____ accreditation organizations. These were given the responsibility of accrediting DMEPOS under Medicare Part B.
    A. 10   B. 15   C. 20   D. 25

    25.____

KEY (CORRECT ANSWERS)

1.	A	11.	D
2.	C	12.	B
3.	C	13.	C
4.	B	14.	D
5.	B	15.	C
6.	B	16.	C
7.	C	17.	A
8.	A	18.	A
9.	C	19.	C
10.	B	20.	D

21. A
22. D
23. B
24. C
25. A

EXAMINATION SECTION
TEST 1

DIRECTIONS: Each question or incomplete statement is followed by several suggested answers or completions. Select the one that BEST answers the question or completes the statement. *PRINT THE LETTER OF THE CORRECT ANSWER IN THE SPACE AT THE RIGHT.*

1. Some organizations address the credentialing and privileging of Advanced Practice Professionals in their
   A. rules
   B. regulations
   C. mission statement
   D. bylaws

   1.____

2. The proportion of ambulatory surgical centers which currently require board certification for privileging is
   A. 30%   B. 45%   C. 66%   D. unknown

   2.____

3. Board _____ is an evaluation which is administered by physician specialty boards; it can also be defined as a metric for calculating the competence of physicians.
   A. meeting
   B. newsletters
   C. certification
   D. announcements

   3.____

4. Several recent studies have found a positive association between certification and
   A. quality of care
   B. the compensation physicians receive
   C. the market value of pharmaceuticals
   D. drug delivery

   4.____

5. Originally, the board certification consisted of a single examination. But in the 1970's, certain specialty boards moved toward _____ certificates.
   A. permanent
   B. time limited
   C. expensive
   D. better quality

   5.____

6. Today, all American Board of Medicine Specialties (ABMS) issue only _____ certificates.
   A. time limited
   B. permanent
   C. better quality
   D. expensive

   6.____

7. In the year 2000, about 24 members of the ABMS approved the plan for moving towards a much more comprehensive assessment for certification. This new plan came to be known as
   A. MOC   B. SOC   C. DOC   D. AOC

   7.____

8. Most of the current research on credentialing and privileging is limited to _____ and health plans.
   A. ambulances
   B. dental clinics
   C. hospitals
   D. nursing facilities

9. MOC evaluated the physician competencies in six main areas which include: patient care, medical knowledge, professionalism, interpersonal skills, knowledge, and
   A. compassion
   B. educational records
   C. practice
   D. insights

10. Credentialing is usually considered an expensive process as an average practitioner application may cost the organization an estimated $60 to
    A. $100
    B. $400
    C. $1,250
    D. $1,500

11. Research shows that small hospitals are _____ likely than large hospitals to require board certification.
    A. less
    B. more
    C. equally
    D. highly

12. Board certification has many _____ over the other available measures of competence.
    A. disadvantages
    B. problems
    C. advantages
    D. issues

13. Certification is static, just like residency and fellowship training.
    A. True
    B. False

14. Certification does not include which of the following?
    A. Physician's cognitive expertise
    B. Examination
    C. Patient feedback
    D. Quality improvement training

15. _____ is an important source for verification of information.
    A. Federation of State Medical Boards
    B. American Board of Medical Specialties
    C. American Medical Association
    D. All of the above

16. For each billing code, CMS calculates a weighted average sales price using the Average Sales Price (ASP) data submitted by manufacturers. The manufacturers submit ASP data at the _____-digit National Drug Code (NDC) level.
    A. 7
    B. 9
    C. 11
    D. 14

17. The Physician Referral Law forbids physicians from referring patients to an entity for a _____ in case the physician or a member of his or her immediate family has a financial relationship with the entity, except in certain exceptional cases.
    A. designated health service
    B. preferred health service
    C. both A and B
    D. none of the above

18. Section IV.B.2.a of the SRDP defines the _____ period as the time during which the disclosing party may not have been in compliance with the Physician Self-referral Law.
    A. look forward
    B. look back
    C. move back
    D. move forward

19. A "_____ practice" is a medical practice which comprises two or more physicians who organize to provide patient care services.
    A. patient   B. hospital   C. physician   D. management

20. If an individual has only Medicare Part B, he is not considered to have minimum essential coverage.
    A. True
    B. False

21. Which of the following is a condition which fulfills the term "appropriate transfer."
    A. The patient has been treated and stabilized at the transferring hospital as far as the limits of its capabilities
    B. The weighing process is described in writing by a physician.
    C. The receiving hospital has been contacted and it approves the transfer.
    D. All of the above

22. EMTALA applies only to people without insurance.
    A. True
    B. False

23. The National Committee for Quality Assurance is a _____, not-for-profit organization which has dedicated itself to improving health care quality.
    A. government
    B. semi-government
    C. private
    D. federal

24. Many preventive screening tests, such as colonoscopies, have been shown to _____ disease morbidity and mortality.
    A. increase
    B. inhibit
    C. reduce
    D. none of the above

25. In 2014, the Affordable Care Act will extent Medicaid eligibility to nearly all residents under the age of
    A. 55
    B. 75
    C. 85
    D. none of the above

KEY (CORRECT ANSWERS)

1. D
2. D
3. C
4. A
5. B

6. A
7. A
8. C
9. C
10. B

11. A
12. C
13. B
14. A
15. D

16. C
17. A
18. B
19. C
20. A

21. D
22. B
23. C
24. C
25. D

TEST 2

DIRECTIONS: Each question or incomplete statement is followed by several suggested answers or completions. Select the one that BEST answers the question or completes the statement. *PRINT THE LETTER OF THE CORRECT ANSWER IN THE SPACE AT THE RIGHT.*

1. Physicians who score in the top quartile of credentialing examination are _____ likely to utilize evidence-based practices than others. 1.____
   A. less   B. more   C. equally   D. highly

2. Board certified physicians are at _____ risk of disciplinary action by a state medical board than their counterparts. 2.____
   A. lower
   C. equal
   B. higher
   D. none of the above

3. A 2003 National Gallup Poll of the general public showed that board certification is _____ to patients. 3.____
   A. insignificant
   C. important
   B. of no consequence
   D. trivial

4. _____ has been defined as the minimum level of skill, knowledge, and/or expertise, derived through training and experience, required to safely and proficiently perform a task or procedure. 4.____
   A. Clinical competency
   C. Credentialing
   B. Experience
   D. Privileging

5. When assessing a physician's endoscopic competence, which of the following should be evaluated? 5.____
   A. The physician uses appropriate sedation.
   B. The physician obtains tissue properly.
   C. The physician discusses his findings with patients or their families.
   D. All of the above

6. _____ includes verifying that the practitioner has documentation of appropriate licensure, education, training, and experience. 6.____
   A. Privileging
   C. Clinical competency
   B. Credentialing
   D. Experience

7. Board certificates and medical licenses are sufficient on their own for documenting completion of training. 7.____
   A. True   B. False

8. Re-credentialing is an interval assessment of 8.____
   A. ideas   B. policies   C. competence   D. practices

9. Studies have demonstrated that low procedural volume can be associated with _____ incomplete procedure and complication rates.
   A. lower
   B. higher
   C. insignificant
   D. decreasing

10. The Joint Commission has mandated that endoscopic privileges must be renewed at least every _____ years for hospital-based endoscopy centers.
    A. 2   B. 3   C. 4   D. 5

11. The Joint Commission has mandated that ambulatory endoscopy and surgical centers require renewal at least every _____ years unless state law provides otherwise.
    A. 2   B. 3   C. 4   D. 5

12. In the event that minimal competence cannot be assured, there are several mechanisms available to a privileging body to ensure high-quality medical care, such as
    A. including proctoring
    B. continuing medical education
    C. limitation of privileges
    D. all of the above

13. According to CMS, credentials alone are _____ for privileging.
    A. sufficient   B. insufficient   C. imperative   D. substitute

14. All states do not recognize accreditation as meeting their state health facility licensing regulator requirements.
    A. True
    B. False

15. _____ Guides are health plan specific versions of the HIPAA-adopted standard Implementation Guides which define the requirements of the health plans for different situational data elements, and also provide special instructions about how the health plan is interpreting the HIPAA Implementation Guides.
    A. Implementation
    B. Patient
    C. Companion
    D. Timely

16. The deadline for upgrading to Versions 5010 and D.0 was January 1,
    A. 2000   B. 2005   C. 2010   D. 2012

17. The date of _____ is considered as the date for determining the codes which depend on service data for their validity, in the case of inpatient claims which span multiple service dates.
    A. receiving services
    B. check in
    C. discharge
    D. none of the above

18. In the case of outpatient claims, the date of _____ is considered with the service item at the line level, and is utilized to determine the codes.
    A. rendering services
    B. checking in
    C. reporting
    D. discharging

19. _____ HIPAA operating rules are present which address spend down amounts for Medicaid agencies.
    A. Three
    B. Five
    C. Seven
    D. None of the above

20. The Council for Affordable Quality Healthcare (CAQH) Committee on Operating Rules for Information Exchange (CORE) acts as the operating rules authoring entity for non-retail _____-related eligibility for a health plan and health care claim status standard transactions.
    A. dental surgery
    B. surgery
    C. pharmacy
    D. gynecology

21. An estimated 17 million low-income people are expected to become newly covered under Medicaid by
    A. 2015
    B. 2020
    C. 2025
    D. 2030

22. Beginning in _____, all U.S. citizens and legal residents will be required to maintain minimum coverage or face a penalty.
    A. 2014
    B. 2020
    C. 2025
    D. 2030

23. The U.S. Bureau of Primary Health Care is the agency that oversees all federally qualified health centers.
    A. Health agencies
    B. Patients care
    C. Primary health care
    D. Secondary health care

24. The agency mentioned above is paying for technical assistance and application fees for 500 health centers to achieve medical home recognition through the
    A. NCQA
    B. HFAP
    C. AAHC
    D. CMA

25. In the Multi-Payer Advanced Primary Care Initiative, Medicare has joined Medicaid and private insurers in multi-payer medical home initiatives in _____ states.
    A. six
    B. eight
    C. ten
    D. twelve

KEY (CORRECT ANSWERS)

1.	B		11.	B
2.	A		12.	D
3.	C		13.	B
4.	A		14.	A
5.	D		15.	C
6.	B		16.	D
7.	B		17.	C
8.	C		18.	A
9.	B		19.	D
10.	A		20.	C

21.	B
22.	A
23.	C
24.	A
25.	B

TEST 3

DIRECTIONS: Each question or incomplete statement is followed by several suggested answers or completions. Select the one that BEST answers the question or completes the statement. *PRINT THE LETTER OF THE CORRECT ANSWER IN THE SPACE AT THE RIGHT.*

1. Legally, the _____ is responsible for the conduct of the hospital as an institution.
   A. investor   B. state   C. hospital   D. trustee

   1._____

2. Privileged physicians are _____ to become members of the medical staff.
   A. eligible   B. ineligible   C. authorized   D. unauthorized

   2._____

3. According to the CMS, apart from doctors or physicians, the medical staff can also include those practitioners who are appointed by the
   A. State
   B. federation
   C. governing body
   D. none of the above

   3._____

4. The IRA Form CP575 is a letter generated by the Internal Revenue Service which is delivered by the IRS and grants individuals their
   A. employer identification number
   B. patient identification number
   C. credentialing ID
   D. physician identification number

   4._____

5. The CMS condition of participation on "Medical Staff," at Section 482.22, concerns the organization and _____ of the hospital medical staff.
   A. transparency
   B. accountability
   C. ethical obligations
   D. policies

   5._____

6. CMS first adopted the term "medical staff" in _____ when it began using the term at Section 482.22 in place of "physicians".
   A. 1960's   B. 1980's   C. 1990's   D. 2010

   6._____

7. One of the requirements of the Joint Commission is that the institutions must have a policy guiding referrals for _____ peer review.
   A. primary   B. secondary   C. internal   D. external

   7._____

8. The National Practitioner Data Bank (NPDB) was established by the Health Care Quality Improvement Act and implemented in
   A. 1990   B. 1994   C. 1998   D. 2000

   8._____

9. Federal law requires hospitals to seek information from the BPDB when a physician applies for membership and at least _____ after that.
   A. monthly
   B. yearly
   C. biannually
   D. every 4 years

   9._____

10. There is _____ data on how the information from NPDB is used for credentialing and peer review activities.
    A. enormous   B. sufficient   C. insufficient   D. no

11. The DSM-V was released in May
    A. 2000   B. 2006   C. 2013   D. 2014

12. DSM-IV and DSM-V are HIPAA adopted code sets.
    A. True   B. False

13. The _____ edits always consist of pairs of HCPCS codes and are arranged in two tables.
    A. Outpatient Code Editor   B. Inpatient Code Editor
    C. Correct Coding Initiative   D. all of the above

14. A _____ is a unit of service (UOS) edit for a Healthcare Common Procedure Coding System (HCPCS)/Current Procedural Terminology (CPT) code for services rendered by a single provider/supplier to a single beneficiary on the same date of service.
    A. Medically Unlikely Edit   B. Medically Likely Edit
    C. Medical Service Edit   D. Medical Procedural Edit

15. The Clinical Laboratory Improvement Amendments of _____ (CLIA) established quality standards for all laboratory testing to confirm the accuracy and reliability of patient test results regardless of the location where the test was performed.
    A. 1977   B. 1988   C. 1999   D. 2009

16. If the beneficiary requires medically necessary hospital care that is expected to span _____ or more midnights, then inpatient admission is generally appropriate.
    A. 1   B. 2   C. 3   D. 4

17. Claims at or above _____ where the beneficiary's therapy services have exceeded the threshold cap for the year will require manual medical review.
    A. $1,700   B. $2,300   C. $3,700   D. $4,500

18. Generally, if the physician cannot conclude whether the patient's diagnosis and treatment plan will involve an anticipated length of stay covering 2 or more midnights, the physician will have to continue to treat the beneficiary as
    A. inpatient   B. outpatient
    C. both A and B   D. none of the above

19. _____ are congressionally-mandated financial limitations on various items such as outpatient occupational therapy or physical therapy but exclude the services provided in the hospital outpatient setting.
    A. Therapy caps   B. Payment caps
    C. Limitation caps   D. None of the above

20. On January 2, 2013, President Obama signed into law the American Taxpayer Relief Act of
    A. 2006   B. 2007   C. 2009   D. 2012

21. Since 2000, the number of uninsured Americans has increased by more than 20 percent. It reached approximately _____ million in 2006.
    A. 20   B. 50   C. 70   D. 80

22. Costs of insurance administration are the _____-growing component of U.S. national health expenditures.
    A. fastest   B. slowest   C. moderately   D. invariably

23. Estimates of the American "hidden tax" range from 8.5 percent of premiums nationally to up to 10.6 percent in
    A. New York   B. Texas   C. Mississippi   D. California

24. In the United States, 89 percent of total national health spending is concentrated among the sickest _____ percent of the population.
    A. 5   B. 15   C. 30   D. 40

25. _____ is the sixth leading cause of death in the U.S., mainly due to the complexity of its treatment.
    A. AIDS
    B. Cancer
    C. Heart attack
    D. Diabetes

KEY (CORRECT ANSWERS)

1.	C	11.	C
2.	A	12.	B
3.	C	13.	C
4.	A	14.	A
5.	B	15.	B
6.	B	16.	B
7.	D	17.	C
8.	A	18.	B
9.	B	19.	A
10.	D	20.	D

21.	B
22.	A
23.	D
24.	C
25.	D

TEST 4

DIRECTIONS: Each question or incomplete statement is followed by several suggested answers or completions. Select the one that BEST answers the question or completes the statement. *PRINT THE LETTER OF THE CORRECT ANSWER IN THE SPACE AT THE RIGHT.*

1. ICD-9-CM procedure codes were named as the HIPAA standard code set for _____ hospital procedures. 1.____
   A. outpatient
   B. inpatient
   C. both A and B
   D. none of the above

2. A health care provider may apply for an NPI in a total of _____ alternative ways. 2.____
   A. two   B. three   C. four   D. five

3. _____ may be described as a series of a situational data element, combined with three data elements. Another characteristic is that their match can be found in the electronic remittance advice or ERA. 3.____
   A. National Provider Identifier
   B. EFT
   C. ERN
   D. TRN segment

4. The Medicare Contracting Reform will affect the Medicare Advantage as well as the prescription drug benefit. 4.____
   A. True
   B. False

5. There are two ways of calculating the number of admissions in ED for measures associated with meaningful use objectives. These include the observation services method and the _____ method. 5.____
   A. patient services
   B. all patient visits
   C. all ED visits
   D. alternate services

6. Since the year _____, an EP must have access to Certified EHR Technology at a location to be able to decide whether to include patients seen in locations 50% threshold or not and whether they are eligible for the EHR Incentive Program. 6.____
   A. 2000   B. 2006   C. 2012   D. 2013

7. There is no overall prerequisite under the Medicare and Medicaid EHR Incentive Programs which compels providers to contribute some maximum amount for the EHR technology that they are utilizing. 7.____
   A. True
   B. False

8. For the satisfactory reporting of the 2013 PQRS incentive eligibility, the PQRS _____% performance rule is applicable. 8.____
   A. 0   B. 10   C. 30   D. 60

9. A minimum of _____ denominator-eligible patients must be Medicare Part B Fee-For-Service (FFS) beneficiaries in case the eligible professionals decide to report measures group via the registry method.
   A. 9   B. 10   C. 11   D. 15

10. _____ refers to a known set of identifiers used by either the states or the federal government for the purpose of identifying service providers before the National Provider Identifiers (NPI's) arrive.
    A. LPI   B. PIN   C. OSCAR   D. NSC

11. For identifying pregnant women in the Medicaid Analytic Extract Data, _____ ways are available.
    A. no   B. twelve   C. sixteen   D. twenty

12. The number of Medicaid Covered Inpatient Days are set as _____ for the dual claims for Medicaid as well as Medicare payments. These claims are also known as the IP crossover records.
    A. ten   B. six   C. three   D. zero

13. For those IP records whose Medicaid Covered Inpatient Days data element value is more than _____, the data element value is set as 365.
    A. 360   B. 350   C. 365   D. 366

14. Which of the following is NOT a state participating in the Recovery Audit Prepayment Review Demolnstration?
    A. Florida   B. California   C. Texas   D. Mississippi

15. There are _____ legal requirements for issuance of an Advanced Beneficiary Notice.
    A. two   B. three
    C. four   D. none of the above

16. Before the ATRA, the original Medicare claims for therapy services which were unable to qualify for a coverage exception were rejected as a benefit category denial, and the beneficiary was financially accountable for the _____ services.
    A. covered   B. non-covered
    C. both A and B   D. none of the above

17. Section 1867 of the _____ Act levies certain responsibilities on Medicare-participating hospitals that provide emergency services. This includes the provision of medical screening examinations (MSE) when a request is made for examination or treatment of an emergency medical condition.
    A. Social Security   B. Affordable Care
    C. Labor   D. none of the above

18. EMTALA applies only to participating hospitals or hospitals which have entered into _____ contracts according to which they may receive payment from CMS under the Medicare program.
    A. supplier
    B. receiver
    C. provider
    D. none of the above

    18._____

19. The term _____ in medical terminology, in the case of emergency medical conditions, refers to the fact that there are no chances of any material deterioration of the patient's condition as a result of the transfer or which may occur during the transfer.
    A. active labor
    B. medical condition
    C. stabilized
    D. unstable

    19._____

20. According to the census of primary care workforce in the U.S., the number of physicians was greater than _____ million in 2010.
    A. one
    B. two
    C. three
    D. four

    20._____

21. Is the usage of ANCC and NCCPA board certification as proof of achieving the highest level of education for nurse practitioners and physician assistants an acceptable act?
    A. Yes
    B. No
    C. Yes, if the organization can obtain written confirmation from ANCC or NCCPA
    D. Not if they get written notice from ANCC or NCCPA

    21._____

22. Does the NCQA anticipate the participatory organization to issue peer-related information?
    A. Yes
    B. No
    C. Up to the organization
    D. Up to the patients

    22._____

23. According to the HEDIS 2013 report, during the initiation of AOD treatment indicator, the term "within 14 days of the IESD (inclusive) has been used". What do you suppose is meant by the term "inclusive" used in this statement? That IESD is
    A. 1 day
    B. 0 days
    C. 3 days
    D. 10 days

    23._____

24. Unlike core elements, _____ elements include requirements that must be met even if the organization delegates 100% of its functions.
    A. structural
    B. non-core
    C. non-structural
    D. compulsory

    24._____

25. Patient-Centered Medical Homes transform primary care into what patients want it to be. This includes
    A. enhanced access to care
    B. care continuity
    C. self-management resources
    D. all of the above

    25._____

KEY (CORRECT ANSWERS)

1.	B	11.	A
2.	B	12.	D
3.	D	13.	C
4.	B	14.	D
5.	C	15.	D
6.	D	16.	B
7.	A	17.	A
8.	A	18.	C
9.	C	19.	C
10.	A	20.	B

21. C
22. C
23. A
24. A
25. D

EXAMINATION SECTION

TEST 1

DIRECTIONS: Each question or incomplete statement is followed by several suggested answers or completions. Select the one that BEST answers the question or completes the statement. *PRINT THE LETTER OF THE CORRECT ANSWER IN THE SPACE AT THE RIGHT.*

1. Which of the following patients must seek an accreditation certificate before choosing the health care center?
   A. A 40-year-old man anticipating a surgical procedure of the appendix
   B. A 25-year-old mother seeking a pediatrician for her newborn
   C. A 50-year-old woman suffering from heart problems
   D. All of the above

   1.____

2. An accredited hospital has the authority to
   A. participate in benchmarking studies
   B. provide accreditation to other hospitals
   C. suggest changes in the credentialing system
   D. operate independently in the future

   2.____

3. "Achieving Accreditation" is a quarterly educational program organized by
   A. HFAP   B. NAMSS   C. AAAHC   D. TJC

   3.____

4. According to the AAAHC rules and regulations, which of the following is the CORRECT sequence of steps for accreditation?
   A. Obtain a copy of AAAHC handbook; conduct self-assessment; AAAHC surveyors conduct survey; prepare organization; get the final decision from AAAHC; submit application
   B. Obtain a copy of the AAAHC handbook; conduct self-assessment; submit application; prepare organization; AAAHC conducts survey; get the final decision from AAAHC
   C. AAAHC conducts survey; obtain a copy of the AAAHC handbook; get the final decision from AAAHC; conduct self-assessment; submit application; prepare organization
   D. None of the above

   4.____

5. It is recommended to involve healthcare professionals and administrators to conduct accreditation surveys.
   A. True   B. False

   5.____

6. Accreditation is awarded to those organizations which demonstrate _____ with the accreditation standards and adhere to the policies.
   A. Minimum compliance   B. awareness
   C. substantial compliance   D. ignorance

   6.____

47

7. Compliance of organizations with the accreditation rules and regulations are assessed through one of these means: documented evidence, answers to questions about implementation, and
   A. on-site observations
   B. interviews
   C. both A and B
   D. none of the above

8. The 2014 health plan standards took effect from
   A. December 31, 2013
   B. January 1, 2014
   C. January 5, 2014
   D. January 15, 2014

9. Which of the following must get accredited?
   A. Surgery centers
   B. Retail clinics
   C. Dental group practices
   D. All of the above

10. In the year 2013, AAAHC was approved as the accreditor for Qualified Health Plans at the federal and _____ levels.
    A. regional
    B. international
    C. state
    D. none of the above

11. The term _____ is used by the federal government as a way to recognize private accreditation organizations.
    A. deemed status
    B. credentialing
    C. privileging
    D. standardized

12. In accordance with CMS policies, it takes approximately _____ days to get an NPI number.
    A. 5
    B. 10
    C. 15
    D. 25

13. Organizations such as AAAHC have the authority to conduct a "deemed status" survey.
    A. True
    B. False
    C. True for dental practitioners only
    D. False for dental practitioners only

14. CMA has established an internet-based system known as _____ as an alternative to the paper enrollment process (CMS-855).
    A. PICOS
    B. SCO
    C. PECOS
    D. PICO

15. Section 301 of the No Fear Act requires each federal agency to post summary _____ data pertaining to complaints of employment discrimination filed against it by employees, former employees and applicants for employment under 29 CFR (Code of Federal Regulations) Part 1614.
    A. statistical
    B. qualitative
    C. experimental
    D. argumentative

16. According to the Medicaid and CHIP April 2014 enrollment data reports, the total number of individuals enrolled is approximately _____ million.
    A. 50
    B. 65
    C. 70
    D. 75

17. In response to the growing number of advisory committees, Congress enacted the _____ which established the guidelines under which all Federal advisory committees must operate.
    A. CMS   B. AAAHC   C. FACA   D. TJC

18. _____ refers to any employee who, by agency regulation, instruction, or other issuance, has been delegated authority to make any determination, give any approval, or take any other action required or permitted by this part with respect to another employee.
    A. Agency   B. Agency ethics
    C. Agency RO   D. Agency designee

19. As required by Sections 2638.201 and 2638.202(b) of CMS guidelines, each agency has a designated _____ who, on the agency's behalf, is responsible for coordinating and managing the agency's ethics program, as well as an alternate.
    A. agency ethics official   B. ethics manager
    C. officer   D. senior ethics manager

20. In accordance with CMS guidelines, an employee shall not accept a gift, directly or indirectly, if it is from a _____ source, or given because of the employee's official position.
    A. prohibited   B. loan   C. gift   D. pension

21. _____ is defined as "any reference to an individual's substance abuse problem or a condition which results from such abuse which is made for the purpose of treatment."
    A. Drug abuse   B. Alcohol abuse
    C. Diagnosis   D. Information

22. _____ means "a communication of patient identifying information or the communication of information from the record of an identified patient."
    A. Diagnosis   B. Informant
    C. Program   D. None of the above

23. In case of a patient who is incapable of managing his own health care decisions, a guardian authorized under the _____ law may act on his behalf.
    A. state   B. national
    C. international   D. none of the above

24. For disclosures with the patient's consent, the written form must contain the
    A. name of the person making the disclosure
    B. date of signing the consent
    C. date on which the consent expires
    D. all of the above

25. For the purpose of preventing multiple enrollments in maintenance treatment programs, which of the following is the CORRECT definition of the term "Central Registry."
    A. The patient identifying information from various sources
    B. A record of drugs used for treating patients
    C. A registry containing information on the expenses of the organization
    D. None of the above

25.____

KEY (CORRECT ANSWERS)

1.	D		11.	A
2.	A		12.	B
3.	C		13.	A
4.	B		14.	C
5.	A		15.	A
6.	C		16.	B
7.	C		17.	C
8.	B		18.	D
9.	D		19.	A
10.	C		20.	A

21. C
22. D
23. A
24. D
25. A

TEST 2

DIRECTIONS: Each question or incomplete statement is followed by several suggested answers or completions. Select the one that BEST answers the question or completes the statement. *PRINT THE LETTER OF THE CORRECT ANSWER IN THE SPACE AT THE RIGHT.*

1. _____ are the minimum health and safety requirements for operation of Medicare certified ASC's.
   A. Coverage conditions
   B. Conditions for coverage
   C. Required conditions
   D. Standard conditions

   1.____

2. According to the recent CMS updates, those members of Medicare program who applied before _____ must revalidate their enrollment under the new criteria of the Affordable Care Act.
   A. March 25, 2009
   B. March 25, 2010
   C. March 25, 2011
   D. March 25, 2012

   2.____

3. Organizations are now required to design an appropriate emergency equipment plan based on the procedures performed and
   A. populations served
   B. staff hired
   C. investors attracted
   D. students enrolled

   3.____

4. The Medicare enrollment application is also called CMS-
   A. 844A
   B. 844B
   C. 855A
   D. 855B

   4.____

5. If an ASC is denied the Medicare certification, it must request the CMS _____ for a written authorization if it wishes an organization with a deemed status to conduct a survey.
   A. chairman
   B. regional office
   C. board of trustees
   D. manager

   5.____

6. The state licensure inspections are different from Medicare surveys and are conducted according to the
   A. state requirements
   B. investors wishes
   C. decision of the board of trustees
   D. international standards

   6.____

7. For a Medicare certified organization, acquisition of deemed status is
   A. voluntary
   B. compulsory
   C. subject to terms and conditions
   D. indispensable

   7.____

8. The deemed status is not a permanent one, rather it only remains throughout the
   A. six months following accreditation
   B. accreditation term
   C. next 48 weeks
   D. next 58 weeks

   8.____

51

9. The _____ determines the effective date of Medicare certification.
   A. JC B. AAAHC C. CMS D. UHAC

10. According to CMS policies, the deemed status survey is
    A. announced 1 month ahead of the survey
    B. announced 2 months ahead of the survey
    C. announced 1 week ahead of the survey
    D. unannounced

11. For the acquisition of a deemed status, each ASC is allowed up to _____ blackout dates.
    A. 5 B. 10 C. 15 D. 20

12. Health net federal services is a subsidiary of Health Net which was awarded in May 2014 _____ re-accreditation under the health network standards from URAC.
    A. full B. partial C. temporary D. conditional

13. The latest version of URAC accreditation program is version _____ which includes measures which fully address the requirements of the Affordable Care Act 2010.
    A. 6 B. 7 C. 8 D. 9

14. URAC's Health Plan Accreditation Program with measures incorporates key market trends, addresses relevant policy issues, and aligns with the _____ components for accrediting health plans as outlined in the ACA Section 1311 requirements for state exchanges.
    A. seven B. eight C. nine D. ten

15. Alex is an employee of the Mapping Agency and has been invited by the XYZ Association of Environmental Management to give a lecture about his agency's role in the protection of the environment. At the conclusion of his speech, the association presents Alex with a framed map with a market value of $18 and a book about the history of mapping with a market value of $15. Which of these gifts can Alex accept, according to the CMS ethical rules and regulations?
    A. He may accept the map.
    B. He may accept the book.
    C. He may accept the map or the book but not both.
    D. He may accept both.

16. The Deficit Reduction Act (DRA) was signed into law on February 8, _____. This legislation affects many aspects of domestic entitlement programs, including both Medicare and Medicaid.
    A. 2009 B. 2007 C. 2006 D. 2008

17. The Deficit Reduction Act requires that the Comprehensive Medicaid Integrity Plan must be revised every _____ year cycles.
    A. 2 B. 3 C. 4 D. 5

18. The _____ is the first comprehensive Federal strategy to prevent and reduce provider fraud, waste, and abuse in the $300 billion per year Medicaid program.
    A. DRA   B. SIP   C. MIP   D. CMS

    18.____

19. Under the Medicaid Integrity Program, the CMS has two broad responsibilities. Firstly, to hire contractors for reviewing Medicaid activities. Secondly, to provide assistance to _____ in their efforts to combat Medicaid fraud.
    A. states   B. countries
    C. organizations   D. patients

    19.____

20. CMS is also required to report to Congress _____ on the effectiveness of the use of funds appropriated for the MIP.
    A. Biannually   B. Annually
    C. Monthly   D. Every four years

    20.____

21. The criminal penalty for violation of laws regarding privacy of patient information generally is not more than $500 for first-time offenders and _____ for second time or subsequent offenses.
    A. $1,000   B. $2,000   C. $4,000   D. $5,000

    21.____

22. A(n) _____ organization is one which provides services to a program such as finance management or laboratory and has entered into a written agreement with the program.
    A. expert   B. qualified services
    C. expert services   D. multiphase

    22.____

23. A _____ payer is the person who pays for a patient's treatment or diagnosis on the basis of a contract with the patient or patient's family. Or on the basis of the patient's eligibility for federal, local, or state benefits.
    A. third party   B. second party
    C. first party   D. none of the above

    23.____

24. _____ agent is a law officer who gets enrolled in a program to investigate any violation of law.
    A. Deceptive   B. Hidden   C. Enrolled   D. Undercover

    24.____

25. An institution cannot participate in Medicare unless it meets each and every condition or attains substantial compliance with requirements for
    A. SNF's and NF's   B. SMF's and MF's
    C. PNF's and PF's   D. PMF's and PF's

    25.____

KEY (CORRECT ANSWERS)

1.	B		11.	A
2.	C		12.	A
3.	A		13.	B
4.	D		14.	C
5.	B		15.	C
6.	A		16.	C
7.	A		17.	D
8.	B		18.	C
9.	C		19.	A
10.	D		20.	B

21. D
22. B
23. A
24. D
25. A

TEST 3

DIRECTIONS: Each question or incomplete statement is followed by several suggested answers or completions. Select the one that BEST answers the question or completes the statement. *PRINT THE LETTER OF THE CORRECT ANSWER IN THE SPACE AT THE RIGHT.*

1. CAHPS is the acronym for Consumer Assessment of
   A. Health Providers and Systems
   B. Health and Patients Societies
   C. High Pressure Sodium
   D. Heartland Payment Systems

2. Which of the following is a key issue stated in the ACA requirements?
   A. Care coordination
   B. Mental health parity
   C. Reward quality
   D. All of the above

3. In 2014, URAC has launched a new publication called _____ as an update to its previous publication *Medical Home Today*.
   A. The Pulse on Clinical Integration
   B. The Pulse of Medicine
   C. Medicine Tomorrow
   D. Medical Home Pulse

4. URAC is a national accreditation leader, offering over _____ highly regarded accreditation programs that span the healthcare spectrum.
   A. 10   B. 30   C. 70   D. 80

5. A(n) _____ in an independent third-party medical review resource that provides objective medical determinations based on evidence that includes medical reports, health plan guidelines, and evidence-based criteria.
   A. review committee
   B. independent review organization
   C. independent review board
   D. resource review committee

6. There are three steps in the appeal process. A first level internal appeal, second level internal appeal, and a third level _____ appeal.
   A. internal   B. external   C. intermediate   D. tertiary

7. According to Section _____ of NAIC's Uniform Health Carrier External Review Model Act, the IRO's and reviewers are not liable for their determinations.
   A. 10   B. 12   C. 14   D. 16

8. _____ is individually identifiable health information, in any form that is held by a covered entity, provider or business associate about health status, provision or payment for health care.
   A. Resource locator
   B. Protected health information
   C. Protected identity
   D. IRO

9. Incomplete documentation can result in a number of outcomes that are less than optimal for health plans, including
   A. a slower review process
   B. increased administrative costs
   C. increased likelihood of legal action by the consumer
   D. all of the above

10. _____ is a process by which a scholarly work is checked by a group of experts from that field to make sure that it meets the expected standards.
    A. Peer review   B. Expert review
    C. Scholarly check   D. None of the above

11. After receiving the request for external review, the IRO will provide written notice on its decision within _____ days.
    A. 30   B. 35   C. 40   D. 45

12. In case of an expedited review, the IRO will provide written notice on its decision within _____ hours.
    A. 24   B. 48   C. 72   D. 96

13. In case of grandfathered self-insured reviews under the Department of Labor ERISA claims, IRO's have _____ days to render a determination.
    A. 50   B. 60   C. 70   D. 80

14. Clinical reviewers must have clinical experience of _____ years to be qualified as an independent review expert.
    A. 3
    B. 5
    C. 10
    D. all of the above

15. Primarily, it is the responsibility of the _____ to combat Medicaid fraud.
    A. states   B. CMS   C. hospitals   D. physicians

16. The State Medicaid Director provides contact information for State Medicaid Directors for each state, the District of Columbia, and the U.S. Territories
    A. Office of Inspector General   B. State Medicaid Director
    C. Fraud Control Unit   D. none of the above

17. The punishment for a first offense of failure to pay child support includes fine or _____ months in prison, or both.
    A. 2   B. 4   C. 6   D. 8

18. Currently, the Medicaid Fraud Control Unit operates in the District of Columbia and _____ states.
    A. 45   B. 47   C. 48   D. 49

19. CMS employees are allowed to take any type of retaliatory action against any entity raising a complaint, question, or concern.
    A. True   B. False

20. All CMS regulations are subject to the _____, which requires agencies to minimize regulatory burden on small businesses and other small entities.
    A. Regulatory Flexibility Act (RFA)   B. Open Door Forums
    C. Non-retaliation Policy   D. none of the above

21. CORF's is the acronym for _____ Rehabilitation Facilities.
    A. Coordinated   B. Comprehensive Outdoor
    C. Comprehensive Outpatient D. Company

22. The Social Security Amendments of 1972 amended the Medicaid Statute to allow the states the option of covering inpatient psychiatric hospitals services for individuals under the age of
    A. 20   B. 21   C. 22   D. 23

23. In 1984, Congress amended 1905(b), removing the requirement for _____ accreditation and adding the requirement that providers of the psych under 21 benefit meet the definition of a psychiatric hospital under the Medicare program.
    A. JC   B. JCAHO   C. CMS   D. AAAHC

24. The term _____ is used for any non-hospital facility with a provider agreement with a State Medicaid Agency to provide the inpatient services benefit to Medicaid-eligible individuals of the psych under 21 benefit program.
    A. JCAHO   B. PR
    C. PRTF   D. none of the above

25. The _____ is ultimately responsible for administration of Medicaid program.
    A. State Medicaid Agency   B. Joint Commission
    C. Board of Trustees   D. FDA

KEY (CORRECT ANSWERS)

1.	A		11.	D
2.	D		12.	C
3.	A		13.	B
4.	B		14.	D
5.	B		15.	A
6.	B		16.	B
7.	C		17.	C
8.	B		18.	D
9.	D		19.	B
10.	A		20.	A

21. C
22. B
23. B
24. C
25. A

TEST 4

DIRECTIONS: Each question or incomplete statement is followed by several suggested answers or completions. Select the one that BEST answers the question or completes the statement. *PRINT THE LETTER OF THE CORRECT ANSWER IN THE SPACE AT THE RIGHT.*

1. The _____ Pricing Program enables covered entities to stretch scarce Federal resources as far as possible, reaching more eligible patients and providing more comprehensive services.
   A. 340B B. 240B C. 140B D. 440B

   1.____

2. The Title V Maternal and Child Health Program was enacted in the _____ as a part of the Social Security Act and continues to be the nation's oldest Federal/State partnership.
   A. 1920's B. 1930's C. 1940's D. 1980's

   2.____

3. According to future-trending reports, specialty drugs will account for the majority of new drug approvals in the coming years, and they will consume approximately _____ percent of a health plan's drug spending by 2020.
   A. 20 B. 40 C. 80 D. 90

   3.____

4. _____ is the term used for medicinal products made from living organisms.
   A. Biosimilars B. Bionics C. Biologics D. Biogen

   4.____

5. A specialty drug is one which
   A. has its usage initiated by a specialist
   B. requires special handling
   C. requires a high degree of patient management
   D. all of the above

   5.____

6. Up to 69 percent of medication-related hospital admissions are caused by _____, at a cost of more than $100 billion a year.
   A. cancer B. AIDS
   C. poor medication adherence D. heart problems

   6.____

7. _____ is a systematic approach to the collection and verification of a provider's professional qualifications.
   A. Provider credentialing B. Employee credentialing
   C. Privileging D. Provider verification

   7.____

8. The top three results that health plans want their specialty pharmacies to achieve are: a decrease in inappropriate utilization, a reduction in drug acquisition costs, and
   A. increased competition
   B. decreased costs
   C. increased pay for healthcare managers
   D. adherence to persistency

   8.____

9. A recent study from the University of California, Davis, found that three cornerstone elements of the medical home model – comprehensive care, patient-centeredness, and extended office hours – correlate with _____ among patients.
   A. a longer lifespan
   B. increased stress
   C. sleep depravity
   D. increased pay

10. Recent surveys total the number of uninsured individuals in America around approximately _____ million.
    A. 10
    B. 15
    C. 20
    D. 35

11. Nearly 40% of U.S. deaths arise from four preventable issues: unhealthy eating, physical inactivity, smoking, and
    A. alcohol use
    B. drug addiction
    C. exposure to carcinogens
    D. self-medication

12. There were five accredited Comprehensive Wellness (CW) organizations submitting data in 2010, nine accredited CW organizations in 2011, and _____ CW companies in 2012.
    A. five
    B. six
    C. seven
    D. eight

13. _____ is the coordination of patient care across conditions, providers, settings, and time to achieve care that is safe, effective, efficient, and patient focused.
    A. Case management
    B. Community claims
    C. Clinical integration
    D. Comprehensive wellness

14. There are a total of _____ NCQA certification levels which CVO's can earn based on their performance.
    A. five
    B. four
    C. three
    D. two

15. The administrative simplification provisions of the Health Insurance Portability and Accountability Act of 1996 (HIPAA, Title II) require the Department of Health and Human Services (HHS) to adopt national standards for electronic health care transactions and national identifiers for providers, health plans, and
    A. physicians
    B. dentists
    C. employees
    d. employers

16. Section 1886(d) of the Social Security Act sets forth a system of payment for the operating costs of acute care hospital inpatient stays under Medicare Part A (Hospital Insurance) based on prospectively set rates. This payment system is referred to as the
    A. IPPS
    B. PSP
    C. PSI
    D. DRG

17. The base payment rate is divided into a labor-related and _____ share.
    A. labor inclusive
    B. non-labor
    C. labor dependent
    D. independent

18. If a hospital treats a high percentage of low-income patients, it receives a percentage add-on payment applied to the _____-adjusted base payment rate.   18.____
    A. RDG   B. IME   C. IPPS   D. DRG

19. Medicare Part A claims processing contractors, called FI's and MAC's had _____ acute care inpatient hospital claim review responsibility.   19.____
    A. no   B. complete   C. partial   D. absolute

20. The primary review responsibility of RAC's is   20.____
    A. identifying past Medicare FFS improper payments
    B. preventing improper payments
    C. promoting quality of care
    D. educating about quality of care

21. _____ has the responsibility of maintaining death report information provided by the RO.   21.____
    A. CMS-CO   B. CMS-JC   C. CMS-RO   D. CMS-SO

22. Survey protocols and interpretive guidelines are established to provide guidance to   22.____
    A. individuals being surveyed   B. individuals conducting surveys
    C. patients   D. patients' families

23. To certify an SNF or NF, a state surveyor completes at least a _____ survey and a standard survey.   23.____
    A. code of conduct   B. ethics code
    C. life safety code   D. patient safety code

24. A sample size is defined as   24.____
    A. a set of data collected and/or selected from a statistical population by a defined procedure
    B. then act of choosing the number of observations or replicates to include in a statistical sample
    C. the average of the squared differences from the mean
    D. none of the above

25. Between 2002 and 2008, the likelihood that a nursing home would receive at least one health deficiency on a survey increased steadily, from 2009 to 2011, this trend has   25.____
    A. intensified   B. reversed   C. advanced   D. eliminated

KEY (CORRECT ANSWERS)

1.	A	11.	A
2.	B	12.	B
3.	B	13.	C
4.	C	14.	D
5.	D	15.	D
6.	C	16.	A
7.	A	17.	B
8.	D	18.	D
9.	A	19.	A
10.	D	20.	A

21. A
22. B
23. C
24. B
25. B

EXAMINATION SECTION
TEST 1

DIRECTIONS: Each question or incomplete statement is followed by several suggested answers or completions. Select the one that BEST answers the question or completes the statement. *PRINT THE LETTER OF THE CORRECT ANSWER IN THE SPACE AT THE RIGHT.*

1. Which of the following is the definition of "credentialing" according to the Joint Commission?
    A. Granting credentials to professionals
    B. Providing the basis for practice within a defined health care setting
    C. The process of obtaining, verifying, and assessing the qualifications of practitioners seeking to provide care
    D. A piece of information which is transferred from a computer to check whether the user is as he claims or to allow others to see the information

    1.____

2. The MOST important reason for credentialing is
    A. ensuring competition
    B. ensuring patient safety
    C. assessing risks
    D. ensuring adequate pricing strategies

    2.____

3. The Medicare Conditions of Participation or COP's are a part of the code of _____ regulations and are aimed at protecting the health or safety of patients.
    A. regional   B. national   C. state   D. federal

    3.____

4. The reason behind getting accredited is
    A. improving the quality of care
    B. meeting the Medicare requirements
    C. ensuring quality of care
    D. all of the above

    4.____

5. The item reviewed during the physician and dentist credentialing process includes
    A. education and work history
    B. prior disciplinary actions and terminations
    C. board certification
    D. all of the above

    5.____

6. According to legal terminology, _____ is defined as the level at which an average healthcare provider in a community should practice.
    A. credentialing   B. privileging
    C. standard of care   D. deeming

    6.____

7. Which of the following certifications assesses whether medical students from outside the United States are ready to be a part of residency programs in the United States?
   A. AAAHC
   B. ECFMG
   C. CPT
   D. HIPDB

8. _____ can be defined as a professional opinion about the applicant's abilities, character or talents.
   A. Suggestion
   B. Peer opinion
   C. Peer reference
   D. Peer recommendation

9. Which of the following authorizes the verification of an applicant's credentials and experience?
   A. Consent statement
   B. Release statement
   C. Consent and release statements
   D. None of the above

10. The _____ defines a practitioner's scope of practice in any organization.
    A. Medical Professional Privilege
    B. Deliberative Process Privilege
    C. Clinical Client Privilege
    D. Clinical Privilege Delineation

11. The staff's structure of governance is defined by the
    A. governance laws
    B. bylaws
    C. administrative laws
    D. structural laws

12. The Current Procedural Terminology is a widely accepted system which is used to report medical procedures and services to the _____ programs developed by the AMA.
    A. health and developmental
    B. health development
    C. health insurance
    D. none of the above

13. _____ is a legal claim against any organization when it fails to perform its duty and ensure clinical competencies.
    A. Negligence
    B. Negligent Credentialing
    C. Lawsuit
    D. Bylaw

14. _____ is the authority granted to an accrediting organization by the CMS once it is ensured that the organization meets the Federal standards.
    A. Crepitation
    B. Deeming
    C. Accreditation
    D. Privilege

15. Which of the following is an accreditor with deemed status?
    A. JC
    B. URAC
    C. AAAHC
    D. All of the above

16. A _____ practitioner is legally permitted to provide care within the specified scope, even in the absence of supervision.
    A. licensed independent
    B. independent
    C. qualified
    D. experienced

17. In medical terminology, an unexpected event linked with death or a serious injury is known as a _____ event.
    A. sentinel   B. headliner   C. hazardous   D. unexpected

18. The function of an MSO is to
    A. provide patient care
    B. evaluate the quality of care
    C. maintain the MSO
    D. all of the above

19. The organization XYZ has regularly participated in the development, implementation, and assessment of rules and regulations, procedures, etc. and has ensured its cooperation with the accreditation regulatory standards. Such behavior may be termed as
    A. compliance   B. infringement   C. defiance   D. dissension

20. How should a medical staff act and interact in the hospital's activities?
    A. In accordance with its bylaws
    B. In accordance with general standards
    C. As directed by peers
    D. As directed by supervisors

21. The bylaws should be reviewed at least
    A. monthly
    B. annually
    C. biennially
    D. every ten years

22. Why is it important for MSP's to be familiar with the accreditation standards which apply to their organization?
    A. To ensure compliance with these regulations and standards
    B. To ensure that maximum profits can be earned
    C. To ensure that minimum resources are wasted
    D. To get ahead of other competitors

23. The MCO's use _____ instead of bylaws to delineate the required functions.
    A. standards
    B. rules and regulations
    C. policies and procedures
    D. none of the above

24. Which of the following is TRUE when considering informed consent or medical negligence?
    A. The parents may give consent on behalf of their children
    B. Consent must be in writing of the patient
    C. For a claim of negligence to be successful, five points must be demonstrated
    D. For a claim of negligence, two points must be demonstrated

25. A prominent legal case of 1988, known as _____, led to the development of HCQIA.
    A. Patrick v. Burget
    B. Einstein v. Burget
    C. Patrick v. Einstein
    D. Elam v. College

KEY (CORRECT ANSWERS)

1. C
2. B
3. D
4. D
5. D

6. C
7. B
8. C
9. C
10. D

11. B
12. C
13. B
14. B
15. D

16. A
17. A
18. D
19. A
20. A

21. C
22. A
23. C
24. A
25. A

———

TEST 2

DIRECTIONS: Each question or incomplete statement is followed by several suggested answers or completions. Select the one that BEST answers the question or completes the statement. *PRINT THE LETTER OF THE CORRECT ANSWER IN THE SPACE AT THE RIGHT.*

1. Credentialing standards apply to _____ providing care.   1.____
   A. licensed practitioners   B. groups of practitioners
   C. licensed or group of practitioners   D. none of the above

2. A practitioner who practices exclusively within an inpatient setting must be credentialed.   2.____
   A. True   B. False

3. The basic criteria for appointing an individual to medical staff is   3.____
   A. education and training   B. competence and health status
   C. licensure   D. all of the above

4. _____ is a system published by Medicare in 1992 according to which the service payments to physicians are determined by the resource costs for their provision.   4.____
   A. CPCS   B. RBRSS
   C. CPMSM   D. None of the above

5. The requirements which are set forth by organizations and certifying bodies like TJC and NCQA are called _____ criteria.   5.____
   A. external   B. internal   C. inclusive   D. exclusive

6. The _____ criteria includes factors defined by a hospital's staff or board.   6.____
   A. external   B. internal   C. inclusive   D. exclusive

7. Independent practitioners can include individuals from many walks of life such as doctors, dentists, or psychologists, depending on the _____ laws.   7.____
   A. regional   B. state   C. national   D. international

8. If the medical staff wishes to recommend appointment by the governing body, then in accordance with the Medicare requirements, the   8.____
   A. bylaws must describe the required qualifications of the candidate
   B. bylaws must describe the required physical characteristics of the candidate
   C. policies must describe the required qualifications of the candidate
   D. none of the above

9. _____ is a private non-profit organization which was established in 1981 to evaluate the United States residency programs.   9.____
   A. ACGMW   B. CPMSM   C. ACW   D. FPPE

10. The _____ board works with member boards for setting up standards for certification or expertise.
    A. American Board of Accreditation
    B. American Board of Medical Specialties
    C. National Board of Medical Specialties
    D. National Association of Medical Specialties

11. The legal case popularly known as Elam v. College Park hospital case is associated with
    A. anti-competitive peer review   B. negligent care
    C. disruptive behavior   D. negligent credentialing

12. _____ has proposed a bureaucratic structure including division of labor and a chain of command.
    A. Taylor   B. Fayol   C. Weber   D. Williams

13. According to Maslow's hierarchy of needs, individuals are motivated by
    A. lowest level needs   B. highest level needs
    C. love and affection   D. sense of security

14. According to _____, the methods of working should be based on statistical quality control rather than the manager's opinion.
    A. Shewhart   B. Maslow   C. Taylor   D. Phillips

15. A popular tool for organizing tasks in projects is
    A. PERT chart B. histogram C. bar graph D. Gantt chart

16. One of the most widely accepted systems of nomenclature, developed by AMA, which is used to report procedures to insurance programs is
    A. CPT   B. HPT   C. IPT   D. APT

17. The _____ is used to identify a medical provider's scope of practice in any institute.
    A. bylaws   B. clinical privilege delineation
    C. peer review   D. hospital plan

18. _____ is a time limited evaluation of a practitioner's performance when new privileges are granted or concerns are raised about his performance.
    A. OPPE   B. FPPE   C. IPPE   D. SPPE

19. Traditionally, there are five functions of management. These include planning, staffing, directing, controlling, and
    A. delegating B. managing   C. organizing D. teaching

20. Many research proposals include a _____ which shows the anticipated time for completion of tasks and the project.
    A. bar graph   B. histogram C. Gantt chart D. PERT chart

3 (#2)

21. A popularly used diagram for root cause analysis, showing cause and effect is
    A. bar graph
    B. Gantt chart
    C. PERT chart
    D. fishbone diagram

22. The maximum number of individuals which a manager can efficiently overlook is called
    A. span of management
    B. maximum limit of supervision
    C. supervision limit
    D. span of supervision

23. _____ had proposed the seven deadly sins and the fourteen points, which were originally shunned in America.
    A. Deming   B. Taylor   C. Weber   D. Maslow

24. According to the national patient safety goals, patients should be included in the preprocedure verification whenever possible.
    A. True   B. False

25. According to the CMS, all Medicare beneficiaries, who are inpatients, must provide an IM from Medicare within _____ day(s) of checking in.
    A. 1   B. 2   C. 3   D. 4

KEY (CORRECT ANSWERS)

1.	C	11.	D
2.	B	12.	C
3.	D	13.	A
4.	D	14.	C
5.	A	15.	A
6.	B	16.	A
7.	B	17.	B
8.	A	18.	B
9.	A	19.	C
10.	B	20.	C

21. D
22. D
23. A
24. B
25. B

TEST 3

DIRECTIONS: Each question or incomplete statement is followed by several suggested answers or completions. Select the one that BEST answers the question or completes the statement. *PRINT THE LETTER OF THE CORRECT ANSWER IN THE SPACE AT THE RIGHT.*

1. Office of _____ is the agency responsible for ensuring privacy and safety of patients, as stated by HIPAA laws.
   A. Privacy Protection
   B. Healthcare Rights
   C. Civil Rights
   D. none of the above

   1._____

2. Which of the following is a type of lawsuit linked with defamation because of incorrect allegations broadcasted through the internet?
   Tort Law –
   A. Libel
   B. Intentional
   C. Negligence
   D. Liability

   2._____

3. Under the HCQIA rules, the adverse action reports should be submitted to state licensing boards within _____ days following the decision.
   A. 10
   B. 15
   C. 20
   D. 25

   3._____

4. Once the adverse action reports have been submitted, the state licensing board must report to the NPDB within the next _____ days.
   A. 5
   B. 15
   C. 25
   D. 35

   4._____

5. The Fourteenth Amendment and Section 1983 fail to provide relief for an individual's private conduct.
   A. True
   B. False

   5._____

6. Which of the following is an INCORRCT way of disposing of data related to the applicant?
   A. Shredder
   B. Incineration
   C. Placing in dumpster
   D. None of the above

   6._____

7. _____ Health Information refers to any information which can be used to identify an individual and determine appropriate care. It may also be used in research studies.
   A. Special
   B. Exposed
   C. Identity
   D. Protected

   7._____

8. The national provider identifier was defined under the HIPAA Act of
   A. 1996
   B. 1998
   C. 2000
   D. 2002

   8._____

9. Physicians with hospital privileges must participate in what the HIPAA privacy rules describe as _____, so they may import information for healthcare activities without violating or entering any agreements.
   A. ACGMW
   B. CPMSM
   C. OHCA
   D. FPPE

   9._____

10. _____ refers to the document prepared by an attorney for appear in a case.
    A. Subpoena   B. Appeal   C. Contract   D. Brief

11. According to the Safe Medical Devices Act of 1990, the staff must report device-related death to the FDA and the
    A. device manufacturer   B. patient's family
    C. police   D. media

12. ECFMG stands for the Electronic Commission for
    A. Foreign Medical Growth   B. Fortescue Medical Graduates
    C. Foreign Medical Graduates   D. Fund Management Groups

13. According to HIPAA, the _____ entities includes those providers who conduct their transactions electronically.
    A. covered   B. E
    C. business   D. digitally connected

14. HIPAA was established in the year _____, following approval by Congress.
    A. 1992   B. 1994   C. 1996   D. 1998

15. The _____ Code is made up of 10 numbers and helps facilitate billing digitally.
    A. Taxonomy   B. Bar   C. Electronic   D. PIN

16. HIPDB started accepting reports in
    A. 1991   B. 1993   C. 1996   D. 1999

17. Since the year _____, NPDB has allowed practitioners to add their own statements to their reports and these may be disclosed to queries.
    A. 2001   B. 2004   C. 2009   D. 2012

18. The U.S. Constitution passed in 1789 has been amended _____ times.
    A. 23   B. 25   C. 27   D. 29

19. A _____ law is the one passed by Congress.
    A. national   B. civil   C. common   D. statutory

20. It is important to inform inpatients and outpatients of their rights.
    A. True   B. False
    C. True for inpatients only D. True for outpatients only

21. Which of the following is NOT to be included in the hospital's written notice to the patient in response to grievances?
    A. Corrective action against employees
    B. Completion date
    C. Investigation steps
    D. Names of associated individuals

22. According to CMS, a time frame of _____ days is considered appropriate for responding to a patient's grievances.
    A. 5 B. 6 C. 7 D. 8

23. The responsibility of addressing grievances with responsibility falls on the _____ of the hospital.
    A. governing body
    B. trustees
    C. manager
    D. investors

24. The quality assessment and performance improvement program must be updated with patient complaints and the data collected in this regard.\
    A. True B. False

25. The complaint of a patient rises to the level of a grievance when it is
    A. not resolved by the staff
    B. postponed for later
    C. made in writing
    D. all of the above

KEY (CORRECT ANSWERS)

1.	C	11.	A
2.	A	12.	C
3.	B	13.	A
4.	B	14.	C
5.	A	15.	A
6.	C	16.	D
7.	D	17.	B
8.	A	18.	C
9.	C	19.	D
10.	D	20.	A

21.	A
22.	C
23.	A
24.	A
25.	D

TEST 4

DIRECTIONS: Each question or incomplete statement is followed by several suggested answers or completions. Select the one that BEST answers the question or completes the statement. *PRINT THE LETTER OF THE CORRECT ANSWER IN THE SPACE AT THE RIGHT.*

1. _____ law is a type of civil law, an example of its violation could be medical negligence.
   A. Tort   B. Public   C. Employment   D. Contract

   1._____

2. In which of the following cases was an organization excused for negligent credentialing as the state granted immunity to nonprofit health.
   A. Harrel v. Total Health Care (1999)
   B. Harrel v. Total Health Care (1989)
   C. Bell v. Sharp Cabrillo Hospital (1989)
   D. Bell v. Sharp Cabrillo Hospital (1999)

   2._____

3. _____ oversees the Institutional Review Boards.
   A. FDA   B. CMH   C. CMS   D. AAAHC

   3._____

4. In accordance with the ADA Law of _____, individuals with disabilities must be granted access to public places.
   A. 1996   B. 1994   C. 1992   D. 1990

   4._____

5. _____ was designed with the aim of preventing hospitals from refusing to treat patients simply based on the source of their payment.
   A. NCQA   B. EMTALA   C. AAAHC   D. HFAP

   5._____

6. The NPDB querying and reporting requirements apply to
   A. dentists
   B. physicians
   C. licensed practitioners
   D. all of the above

   6._____

7. Which of the following may NOT query at the NPDB?
   A. Medical malpractice payers
   B. Health care practitioners
   C. Professional societies
   D. State Licensing Boards

   7._____

8. _____ is an updated version of CFR and an editorial compilation of its material. It is updated on a regular basis.
   A. e-CRR   B. e-CMR   C. e-CFR   D. CMR

   8._____

9. The NPDB – HIPDB allows self-query by applicants even in the absence of a signed and notarized paper copy submitted to the data banks.
   A. True   B. False

   9._____

10. Hospitals are not required to query more than once every _____ years on a continuous staff practitioner.
    A. 5   B. 4   C. 3   D. 2

    10._____

73

11. The _____ processes the information as submitted by the reporting entity to the NPDB.
    A. IPRS B. IQRS C. IMRS D. ISRS

12. According to the NPDB research statistics, the number of adverse action reports in the U.S. between 2002 and 2012 is around
    A. 650,000 B. 550,000 C. 450,000 D. 350,000

13. The _____ Act was passed in 1946 and provides subsidies for expansion of hospitals in exchange for the provision of free care.
    A. Assistance
    B. Henry Burton
    C. Hill Burton
    D. none of the above

14. The pre-employment medical examinations have been prohibited by the Americans with Disabilities Act of
    A. 19990 B. 1992 C. 1996 D. 1998

15. _____ is a federal law which requires healthcare facilities receiving state funds to provide information about advanced directives to patients in the form of written material.
    A. COBRA B. COBRA-II C. PRDA D. PSDA

16. An amendment to the Social Security Act in 1965 led to the establishment of
    A. affordable care
    B. insurance
    C. Medicare
    D. Social Security

17. The URAC accreditation program is four phased. These include the application building, desktop review, onsite review, and _____ review.
    A. committee B. application C. standard D. enhanced

18. In 2013, in response to the ACA mandate for consumer friendly health plan data, URAC constructed the URAC _____ system.
    A. friendly data
    B. data
    C. star data
    D. consumer's data

19. _____, 1986, is a federal law which was enacted to create a national tracking system of physicians with records of malpractice.
    A. EMTALA B. HCQIA C. AAAHC D. NCB

20. HCQIA provides immunity from civil money damages in peer review cases, but an exception to this is the damages related to
    A. those who misreport to the review body
    B. those who provide false information
    C. civil rights action
    D. all of the above

21. EMTALA is also known as
    A. COBRA
    B. Patient Anti-dumping Law
    C. both A and B
    D. none of the above

22. EMTALA does not apply to the transfer of stable patients. 22.____
    A. True B. False

23. CMS and OIG have powers regarding violation of EMTALA and these can include hospital fines of up to 23.____
    A. $90,000 B. $80,000 C. $60,000 D. $50,000

24. In 2014, a chair of AAAHC, _____, has been selected to represent AAAHC on the Affordable Care Act advisory panels. 24.____
    A. Mark Brown B. Karren Conolly
    C. Patrick Daves D. Ira Cheifetz

25. An organization's emergency management plan, according to the Joint Commission, must include 25.____
    A. civil disasters B. criminal acts
    C. biological disaster D. all of the above

KEY (CORRECT ANSWERS)

1.	A		11.	B
2.	B		12.	D
3.	A		13.	C
4.	D		14.	A
5.	B		15.	D
6.	D		16.	C
7.	A		17.	A
8.	C		18.	C
9.	B		19.	B
10.	D		20.	D

21. C
22. A
23. D
24. B
25. D

EXAMINATION SECTION
TEST 1

DIRECTIONS: Each question or incomplete statement is followed by several suggested answers or completions. Select the one that BEST answers the question or completes the statement. *PRINT THE LETTER OF THE CORRECT ANSWER IN THE SPACE AT THE RIGHT.*

1. A person with incomplete staff privileges who is in the transition from provisional active status is termed

    A. attending
    B. associate
    C. courtesy
    D. consulting

2. Which of the following is an advantage associated with the use of a prime vendor in hospital materials management?

    A. Lower in-hospital inventory levels
    B. Consistent product quality
    C. Strict price controls
    D. Heightened competition

3. Which of the following is NOT typically a function of a hospital CEO?

    A. Negotiating with third-party payors
    B. Functioning in a judgmental or deliberative fashion
    C. Reviewing and establishing hospital procedures
    D. Managing the hospital's assets

4. Hospital finance documents may occasionally provide for a *basket,* which is a(n)

    A. maintenance test whereby the hospital agrees to set its rates so as to generate sufficient revenues to pay the debt service on a bond
    B. letter of credit from an AA or AAA-rated bank, or a municipal bond insurance policy issued by an AAA-rated insurance company
    C. minimum level of debt that can be incurred without the need of meeting any financial performance tests
    D. asset-based covenant associated with a taxable bond

5. Medicare's Preferred Provider System (PPS) applies to
    I. rehabilitation hospitals
    II. children's hospitals
    III. adult acute-care hospitals
    IV. competitive medical plans

    The CORRECT answer is:

    A. I, III B. II, III C. III *only* D. II, IV

6. Generally, the most basic function of a management services organization (MSO) is to act as a vehicle for

    A. vertical integration
    B. managed care contracting
    C. quality control
    D. utilization review

7. The _____ committee(s) is(are) mandated at all hospitals by the Joint Commission on the Accreditation of Health Care Organizations (JCAHO).
   I. executive
   II. ethics
   III. credentials
   IV. surgical review

   The CORRECT answer is:

   A. I only
   B. I, III, IV
   C. II, IV
   D. II, III

8. Which of the following general statements about the work force in United States hospitals is FALSE?
   It is

   A. more organized by unions than most general industries
   B. highly integrated by function and occupation
   C. predominantly female
   D. comparatively young

9. In the average United States hospital, the Medicare program accounts for about _____ % of all revenues.

   A. 20
   B. 40
   C. 60
   D. 80

10. In inpatient community hospitals, which of the following utilization trends has increased over the past few years?

    A. Length of stay
    B. Inpatient admissions
    C. Inpatient days
    D. Beds

11. Each of the following was a characteristic of the health care industry at the turn of the 20th century EXCEPT

    A. competition
    B. freedom from regulation
    C. nursing glut
    D. provider oversupply

12. The FIRST step in a hospital's attempt to contain labor costs should most likely be to

    A. replace labor with lesser-skilled personnel
    B. increase productivity
    C. replace labor with nonlabor (i.e., automated) expenditures
    D. reduce the demand for particular services

13. Which of the following is NOT a typical subsystem associated with hospital food service systems?

    A. Safety
    B. Menu planning
    C. Maintenance
    D. Distribution/service

14. In multiprovider systems, the MAIN advantage to using the corporate structure in governance is that

    A. there is greater systemwide access to the expertise of advisers
    B. institutions have greater autonomy in their own operation

C. risk is tightly controlled
D. the lines of authority are clear

15. In a typical hospital organization, which of the following departments serves as the foundation for medical records?

    A. Environmental Services
    B. Nursing
    C. Accounting
    D. Admitting/Patient Access Services

16. In productivity improvement, which of the following procedures is typically performed first?

    A. In-depth studies   B. Productivity reporting
    C. Management orientation   D. Quality control

17. The most traditional — and generally least effective — means of distributing hospital materials is through

    A. point-of-use replenishment systems
    B. PAR-level systems
    C. exchange carts
    D. requisitions

18. Factors to consider in developing the range of testing performed by a hospital laboratory fall into four general categories. Which of the following is NOT one of these?

    A. Legal or professional requirements
    B. Patient flow
    C. Technical and personnel capabilities
    D. Medical needs

19. Which of the following is an external *input* stakeholder in a hospital?

    A. Managers   B. Competitors
    C. Support personnel   D. Third-party payers

20. Medicare's PPS payments are made on a _____ basis.

    A. fee-for-service   B. charge
    C. per diem rate   D. per-discharge

21. The strategic planning process at a hospital often begins with a *plan to plan*. Which of the steps in this process is typically performed FIRST?

    A. Assessing internal and external environments
    B. Formulating strategic options
    C. Developing an implementation schedule
    D. Developing organizational goals

22. Medicare's DRG payment rates represent full payment to a hospital for all inpatient hospital costs EXCEPT

    A. capital-related costs   B. ancillary services
    C. routine care   D. special care units

23. Which of the following has been a trend in hospital care since 1980?   23.___
    A

    A. 5% increase in inpatient visits
    B. 10% decline in both hospitals and beds
    C. 10% increase in outpatient visits
    D. 20% increase in trauma care center activity

24. Factors which inhibit the vertical integration of multihospital systems involve each of the   24.___
    following EXCEPT

    A. physician resistance
    B. government scrutiny
    C. administrative costs
    D. the movement of sick people through a dispersed system of care

25. Approximately what percentage of a hospital's budget is related to materials, equipment,   25.___
    and purchased services?

    A. 1-10   B. 10-20   C. 30-50   D. 50-70

KEY (CORRECT ANSWERS)

1. B		11. C	
2. A		12. D	
3. B		13. A	
4. C		14. D	
5. C		15. D	
6. B		16. C	
7. A		17. D	
8. B		18. B	
9. C		19. D	
10. B		20. D	

21. A
22. A
23. B
24. C
25. C

TEST 2

DIRECTIONS: Each question or incomplete statement is followed by several suggested answers or completions. Select the one that BEST answers the question or completes the statement. *PRINT THE LETTER OF THE CORRECT ANSWER IN THE SPACE AT THE RIGHT.*

1. Of the following, which area represents the greatest difference between the operations of free-standing hospitals and multi-provider systems?

    A. Financial management
    B. Marketing
    C. Risk management
    D. Information systems

2. The medical record of a hospital patient

    A. is the property of the patient and may not be used for purposes other than diagnosis, treatment or quality review without the expressed consent of the patient
    B. is the property of the hospital, which has the obligation to safeguard it from unauthorized use, loss, or destruction
    C. is jointly owned by both the patient and the institution, and is not accessed or released without appropriate consent
    D. becomes the property of the state upon the patient's discharge, and is subject to all applicable regulations regarding access and use

3. Which of the following types of tests is subject to the federal regulations regarding clinical laboratories?

    A. Testing in physician office laboratories
    B. Research testing for which patient-specific results are not reported
    C. Drug testing performed by NIDA-certified laboratories
    D. Testing for forensic purposes

4. Currently, outpatient service accounts for an average of about _____ % of a hospital's total revenue.

    A. 15   B. 30   C. 50   D. 65

5. What type of medical record emphasizes chronological entry?

    A. Problem-oriented
    B. Quantitative
    C. Source-oriented
    D. Integrated

6. The rapid growth of ambulatory services, and the accompanying movement toward free-standing and independently owned facilities, has been driven by each of the following factors EXCEPT

    A. payor pressure to check costs
    B. outdated inpatient facilities
    C. increased reimbursement availability
    D. state CON legislation

7. In a typical hospital pharmacy department, drug expenditures generally account for about _____ % of the operating budget.

    A. 30   B. 50   C. 70   D. 90

8. A significant advantage to the team approach to hospital design and construction is that

   A. planning and construction times are minimized
   B. the process is sequential
   C. relative building quality is usually higher than in the traditional method
   D. the project is bid on a lump-sum basis

9. In a hospital's administrative structure, a span of control of about _____ in a given functional area is normal to achieve optimal effectiveness.

   A. 2-4   B. 3-7   C. 5-10   D. 8-15

10. The largest portion of financing for nonprofit hospitals generally comes from _____ bonds.

    A. tax-exempt local authority
    B. taxable municipal
    C. minimum-tax state government
    D. tax-exempt state agency

11. In a hospital, the easiest and least costly fire prevention/safety provision that can be made is to

    A. install effective fire detection systems
    B. comply with appropriate construction codes and standards
    C. implement a staff response training program
    D. eliminate the cause of fire occurrences

12. In the past two decades, which of the following has done the most to diminish horizontal integration strategies among multiprovider systems?

    A. The aging population
    B. Greater differentiation in strategies
    C. The implementation of PPS
    D. Local and regional orientation

13. Which of the following is NOT a significant factor in the changing reimbursement policies of United States hospitals?

    A. The shift to prospective hospital reimbursement
    B. Increasingly aggressive utilization review policies of third-party reimbursers
    C. Increased use of capitation payment
    D. Expanded referral bases

14. The quality improvement process

    A. is a way of taking action to improve problems
    B. is designed to realign processes
    C. delegates responsibility to a few key managers
    D. establishes performance thresholds

15. The driving force behind strategic thinking, planning, and managing in hospitals should always be the

    A. hospital's mission
    B. hospital's profit margin
    C. external environment
    D. satisfaction of stakeholders

16. _____ costs are excluded from Medicare's diagnosticrelated group (DRG) payment rates.

    A. Stepped-down   B. Pass-through
    C. Privileged   D. Outlying

17. Which of the following is a financing instrument that provides a mechanism for consolidating the credit of the participating corporations, and for developing a legal framework for the future borrowings of each department?

    A. Variable rate demand bond (VRDB)
    B. Master indenture
    C. Equity financing
    D. Rate covenant

18. The ultimate purpose of general cost-finding is to

    A. recast or reclassify the costs accumulated in the routine accounts
    B. differentiate between fixed and variable costs
    C. determine the full costs of operating the revenue-producing centers of the hospital
    D. determine an appropriate fee for certain services

19. Which of the following was a common characteristic on the internal environment of United States hospitals prior to 1965?

    A. Stable costs
    B. Outdated facilities
    C. Slow growth
    D. Increasing personnel specialization

20. In writing job descriptions, a human resources staff member should generally adhere to each of the following guidelines EXCEPT

    A. use qualitative rather than quantitative words when possible
    B. determine or estimate the percentage of time spent on each activity
    C. start each section with an active functional verb in the present tense
    D. state separate duties clearly and concisely, without excess detail

21. A hospital can improve its return on assets (ROA) by
    I. increasing profit margin
    II. increasing asset turnover
    III. decreasing asset commitments
    The CORRECT answer is:

    A. I only   B. III only   C. II, III   D. I, II, III

22. In a typical hospital organization, which of the following is part of the ancillary services department?

    A. Admitting
    B. Pharmacy
    C. Medical records
    D. Central supply

23. The PRIMARY advantage associated with a pooled hospital financing program is that

    A. the hospital will not be required to show a letter of credit in order to participate
    B. the hospital can arrange for financing that suits its particular circumstances
    C. liability is distributed among pool members
    D. a hospital may participate in financing that has already been structured

24. A hospital learns that its employees have initiated the unionization process. Under federal law, the hospital is prohibited from

    A. discussing the impact of union dues and the general costs of individual membership
    B. preventing solicitation of membership during working hours
    C. granting wage increases or special concessions during the election
    D. communicating its reasons for opposition to recognition of the union

25. For a public hospital, an investment-interests *safe harbor* can exist if

    A. the hospital has undepreciated net tangible healthcare assets of at least $20 million
    B. the investment represents the purchase of a federally-registered security
    C. the investment is achieved through a loan or guaranty by the entity in which the investment is made
    D. marketing of items or services is directed exclusively at investors

KEY (CORRECT ANSWERS)

1.	A	11.	D
2.	B	12.	C
3.	A	13.	D
4.	B	14.	B
5.	D	15.	A
6.	B	16.	B
7.	C	17.	B
8.	A	18.	C
9.	C	19.	D
10.	D	20.	A

21.	D
22.	B
23.	D
24.	C
25.	B

TEST 3

DIRECTIONS: Each question or incomplete statement is followed by several suggested answers or completions. Select the one that BEST answers the question or completes the statement. *PRINT THE LETTER OF THE CORRECT ANSWER IN THE SPACE AT THE RIGHT.*

1. Which of the following is most widely accepted as the required academic preparation for health administration?

    A. Bachelor's degree
    B. Master's degree
    C. Ph.D.
    D. M.D.

2. Management engineering in hospitals can be used for each of the following purposes EXCEPT

    A. providing a resource standard as a basis for a cost-accounting system
    B. structuring job evaluation procedures according to productivity measures
    C. providing a productivity management system to monitor resource utilization
    D. reducing the costs of present operations

3. Approximately what percentage of all energy consumed by a hospital is used in the heating, ventilating, and air conditioning (HVAC) systems?

    A. 20   B. 40   C. 60   D. 80

4. In the general physical planning of a health care facility, certain interdepartmental relationships should be considered. Which of the following is generally the most important relationship to preserve in the facility's design?

    A. Pharmacy/Materials management
    B. Laboratory/Emergency
    C. Radiology/Pharmacy
    D. Education/Medical

5. Typically, the clinical information department in a hospital is responsible for transcribing
    I. autopsy protocols
    II. interpretations of graphic data (EEC, EKG, etc.)
    III. discharge summaries
    IV. x-ray reports

    The CORRECT answer is:

    A. I, II, IV
    B. II, III
    C. III, IV
    D. I, II, III, IV

6. In forming a nonprofit foundation, which of the following is typically done FIRST?

    A. Performing due diligence
    B. Appraising physician compensation
    C. Preparing an asset purchase agreement
    D. Defining finance options

7. In the job analysis process in hospitals, which of the following is LEAST likely to be used as a means of obtaining information about jobs?

   A. Personal observation of the actual performance of a job by a job analyst
   B. Interviews conducted by job analysis
   C. Published abstracts of job content at similar institutions
   D. Incumbent questionnaires

8. The ambulatory patient grouping (APG) system of reimbursement is based on the payment unit of the

   A. day of care
   B. individual procedure
   C. straight charge
   D. outpatient visit

9. In which of the following radiology divisions is central scheduling likely to be LEAST effective?

   A. Radiation therapy
   B. Angiography
   C. Ultrasound
   D. Mammography

10. In hospital management engineering, the primary objective of layout and equipment studies is to

    A. reduce walking distances and total labor input
    B. increase patient throughput
    C. achieve the correct balance between span of control and delegation of responsibility
    D. improve the flow of information

11. Which of the following agencies is responsible for issuing certification documents or waivers for testing done at clinical laboratories?

    A. Occupational Safety and Health Administration (OSHA)
    B. American Medical Association (AMA)
    C. Health Care Finance Administration (HCFA)
    D. Joint Commission on the Accreditation of Health Care Organizations (JCAHO)

12. Which of the following is a process-of-care measure of quality for a hospital?

    A. Compliance with discharge plan
    B. Postdischarge events
    C. Complications
    D. Communication between clinical staff

13. In the most widely accepted model for strategic stakeholder management in hospitals, which of the following steps should be performed FIRST?

    A. Identifying which internal stakeholders should be involved in the implementation process
    B. Diagnosing each stakeholder in terms of potential for threat and potential for cooperation
    C. Evaluating the effective managerial implications of effectively managing stakeholders from a strategic point of view
    D. Formulating generic stakeholder management strategies

14. The most common reimbursement method in managed care plans is
    A. straight charges
    B. sliding scale per diem
    C. discount on charges
    D. fee-for-service

15. At what level of a hospital's medical staff membership is a person who does not frequently admit patients and who does not have the full obligations of active staff membership?
    A. Provisional
    B. Consulting
    C. Courtesy
    D. Temporary

16. In the development of a new health care facility, or of an addition to an existing facility, which of the following procedures in the implementation process is typically performed FIRST?
    A. Equipment planning
    B. Preliminary financial feasibility study
    C. Financial strategy development
    D. CON development

17. Which of the following is an advantage associated with the use of consignment buying in hospital materials management?
    A. Flexibility in choosing vendors
    B. Steady vendor inventory levels
    C. Strict price controls
    D. Improved cash flow

18. In general, hospitals today are least likely to offer which of the following benefits to their employees?
    A. Individual medical coverage
    B. Short-term disability coverage
    C. Vision coverage
    D. Pension plan

19. In a hospital's cost finding process, which of the following would be counted as a direct cost?
    A. Laboratory
    B. Administration
    C. Utilities
    D. Dietary

20. Performance evaluations of hospital employees should generally include each of the following EXCEPT
    A. jointly developing a plan of action with the employee
    B. a measurement of the employee's performance against the performance of other employees in the same department
    C. tangible assistance toward the development of the employee
    D. gaining acceptance of the standards expressed at the outset of the evaluation process

21. What is considered to be the basic functional unit in a clinical laboratory? 21.____

    A. Tissue type
    B. Workstation
    C. Relative value unit (RVU)
    D. Test category

22. What is the term for the account group used to record the transactions involving the hospital's investments is land, buildings, and equipment? 22.____

    A. Fixtures
    B. Capital fund
    C. Master indenture
    D. Plant fund

23. The most notable example of a *closed* medical staff within a hospital is in the _____ department. 23.____

    A. emergency
    B. respiratory therapy
    C. radiology
    D. oncology

24. Which of the following is an advantage associated with the formation of a management services organization (MSO)? 24.____

    A. Reduced likelihood for Medicare/Medicaid fraud or abuse
    B. Decreased financial risk
    C. Lower per-physician costs
    D. Tighter hospital control of medical staff

25. Under Medicare regulations, which of the following is eligible for reimbursement as a direct general medical education (GME) cost? 25.____

    A. Faculty salary
    B. Meal costs
    C. Administrative/general service costs
    D. Medical library costs

KEY (CORRECT ANSWERS)

1.	B	11.	C
2.	B	12.	D
3.	C	13.	B
4.	B	14.	D
5.	D	15.	C
6.	B	16.	D
7.	C	17.	D
8.	D	18.	C
9.	B	19.	A
10.	A	20.	B

21. B
22. D
23. C
24. C
25. A

EXAMINATION SECTION
TEST 1

DIRECTIONS: Each question or incomplete statement is followed by several suggested answers or completions. Select the one that BEST answers the question or completes the statement. *PRINT THE LETTER OF THE CORRECT ANSWER IN THE SPACE AT THE RIGHT.*

1. Practical/vocational nursing programs typically range from _____ in length.

    A. 3-6 months
    B. 6-18 months
    C. 1-2 years
    D. 2-3 years

2. According to most practitioners, the most important purpose for the establishment of a classification system for nursing diagnoses is

    A. providing a common reference system to assist in the growth of clinical knowledge through research
    B. assisting computerization of the nursing process
    C. identifying nursing's independent practice domain
    D. meeting and keeping requirements

3. Mr. Johnson is a 55-year-old patient with a CVA who is unable to reposition himself in bed. In order to win a malpractice suit against the nursing staff, he would need to establish that

    A. the nurses intended to cause bodily harm
    B. a felony has been committed against him
    C. sympathetic compatibility was not maintained
    D. his ulcer resulted from lack of care

4. Which of the following is an example of an interdependent nursing action?

    A. Sterile dressing changes
    B. Patient teaching regarding appropriate personal hygiene
    C. The development of a nursing care plan
    D. Preparation for diagnostic tests

5. Which of the following is NOT a purpose of the Americans with Disabilities Act?
   To

    A. establish a board for the administration of specific grievances lodged by individuals with disabilities
    B. ensure that the federal government plays a central role in enforcing standards established under the act
    C. provide a clear and comprehensive national mandate for eliminating discrimination against individuals with disabilities
    D. provide clear, strong, enforceable standards addressing discrimination against individuals with disabilities

6. A person's rights of freedom and choice, which express the right of people to live as they choose within prescribed boundaries, are known as _____ rights.

    A. option   B. welfare   C. inalienable   D. legislative

7. Which of the following recordkeeping practices could NOT be grounds for fraud?

    A. *Whiting out* or obliterating information
    B. Waiting to sign entries until after they can be confirmed by another professional
    C. Failing to write the date and time on an entry
    D. Leaving blank spaces or lines in the record

8. Rural primary care was created in the United States as a result of the _____ Act.

    A. Omnibus Budget Reconciliation   B. Health Maintenance Organization
    C. Rural Health Clinics   D. Smith-Hughes

9. A contract between two parties may be invalid if

    A. the parties to the contract are of legal age to enter into a binding agreement
    B. there is mutual agreement about the service to be provided
    C. the duties to be performed are within the law
    D. there is no promise, implied or otherwise, of compensation for the service to be provided

10. A nurse may

    A. only read patient charts for professional reasons
    B. look at a friend's chart to see the diagnosis
    C. share information from a medical record to protect a friend
    D. share information from a medical record with other nurses under any circumstances

11. The functional mode of nursing care delivery

    A. permits decentralized direction and control
    B. is task-oriented
    C. is designed to respond to the needs of both clients and employees
    D. is often proven to be fiscally irresponsible

12. The MAIN difference between decision-focused and action-focused ethical problems is that

    A. decision-focused problems involve moral distress
    B. action-focused problems cannot be resolved by improving one's decision-making skills
    C. action-focused problems can only be resolved collaboratively
    D. decision-focused problems tend to occur less frequently in nursing situations

13. A nurse may protect him/herself from lawsuits by means of each of the following EXCEPT

    A. demeanor
    B. documentation in the medical record
    C. delegation of riskier tasks
    D. dedication to competency

14. Which of the following is an example of a tertiary health care service?

    A. Services by a cardiologist
    B. Advanced specialized rehabilitative care
    C. Health promotion
    D. Continuing care for common health problems

15. The FIRST stage in the nursing planning phase is

    A. developing outcomes
    B. developing nursing orders
    C. setting priorities
    D. documentation

16. An incident report must always be completed within _____ of an incident or accident occurring at a health care agency.

    A. 12 hours   B. 24 hours   C. 2 days   D. 3 days

17. _____ are written documents that contain rules, policies, procedures, regulations, and orders for the conduct of patient care in various stipulated circumstances that are unique to the agency making them known.

    A. Codes of Ethics
    B. Nurse Practice Acts
    C. Standard Operating Procedures
    D. Standards of Care

18. Because of the changing nature of health care delivery in the United States, consumers have tended to change in each of the following ways EXCEPT

    A. greater knowledge about their health
    B. expectation of playing a role in decision-making concerning treatments
    C. decreasing influence on health care delivery
    D. better awareness of how lifestyle affects health

19. A practical student nurse is educated to understand the concepts of a system of total patient care that considers the physical, emotional, social, economic, and spiritual needs of the person; the person's response to the illness; and the impact of the person"s ability to meet self-care needs.
    The modern nursing practice that expresses the philosophy of this care is

    A. continuity of care
    B. holistic nursing
    C. health care delivery system
    D. wellness/illness continuum

20. A nurse is professionally considered to be an *expert* when

    A. he demonstrates organizational ability
    B. her analytical ability can be transferred to situations with which the nurse has had no previous experience
    C. she has been on the job in a similar situation for two to three years
    D. he uses maxims as guides but applies them only after acquiring a deep understanding of the situation

21. Which of the following is NOT a disadvantage associated with the DRG classification system?
    It

    A. does not provide a measure of the quality of care
    B. often slows the discharge of clients
    C. fails to include all diagnoses and procedures
    D. does not account for advances in diagnostic procedures or therapies

22. Which of the following is a PAST characteristic of nursing practice?

    A. Quasiprofessional status
    B. Planning and cognitive tasks as the major domain
    C. Growth as an independent practice
    D. Constraint of care goals by limited resources as contextual factors

23. The Association of Practical Nursing Schools was founded in

    A. 1892 B. 1907 C. 1941 D. 1961

24. Any form of communication that may injure a person's reputation is known legally as

    A. libel   B. gossip
    C. defamation of character   D. slander

25. The Patient Self-Determination Act requires each of the following from hospitals receiving payment from Medicare and Medicaid EXCEPT

    A. provide staff and community education on advance directives
    B. inform the client regarding the hospital's policy on how advance directives are honored
    C. provide clients with preprinted forms for the type of advance directive requested
    D. provide a written statement on the client's chart indicating whether the client has an advance directive

KEY (CORRECT ANSWERS)

1. B
2. C
3. D
4. C
5. A

6. A
7. C
8. A
9. D
10. A

11. B
12. B
13. C
14. B
15. C

16. B
17. C
18. C
19. B
20. B

21. B
22. A
23. C
24. C
25. C

TEST 2

DIRECTIONS: Each question or incomplete statement is followed by several suggested answers or completions. Select the one that BEST answers the question or completes the statement. *PRINT THE LETTER OF THE CORRECT ANSWER IN THE SPACE AT THE RIGHT.*

1. In 1983, the National League for Nursing voted to retain the _____ as the minimal academic preparation for the professional nurse. 1._____

    A. hospital diploma
    B. associate degree
    C. baccalaureate degree
    D. master's degree

2. If a female nurse is paid less than a male nurse for the same work, the category of collective bargaining that has been breached is 2._____

    A. violations of federal or state law
    B. contract violations
    C. management responsibilities
    D. violation of agency rules

3. Which of the following is NOT a disadvantage associated with the implementation of team nursing? 3._____

    A. Client may perceive care as fragmented
    B. De-emphasizes humanistic values
    C. Inadequate expertise of team members
    D. Leaders often revert to functional care mode

4. Nurses may rely on the rights granted in their respective states to provide them with basic legal protection, but they must operate professionally, prudently, and within the scope of their authority. This provision is in the 4._____

    A. Patient's Bill of Rights
    B. Standards of Care
    C. Nurse Practice Act
    D. Code of Ethics

5. Which of the following is an example of private law affecting nurses? 5._____

    A. Theft
    B. Illegal possession of controlled substances
    C. Child abuse laws
    D. False imprisonment

6. A nurse _____ is a nurse working in an expanded role who has the knowledge and skills necessary to detect and manage limited acute and chronic stable conditions. 6._____

    A. practitioner
    B. clinician
    C. generalist
    D. specialist

7. Each of the following is a basic rule for a nurse to follow in charting a patient EXCEPT
   A. chart the time and method of transportation every time a patient leaves a unit
   B. chart before, during, and after care is given
   C. leave no empty lines
   D. note patient responses to treatments and analgesics or other special medications

8. A nurse who handles a deceased client is encouraged to place identification tags in each of the following locations EXCEPT the
   A. shroud   B. ankle   C. neck   D. wrist

9. The nursing theory involving *unitary man* was developed by
   A. Jung   B. Rogers   C. Roy   D. Orlando

10. Nursing interventions are derived *primarily* from each of the following sources EXCEPT
    A. past nursing experience
    B. intuition
    C. nursing theory based on research
    D. scientific knowledge associated with the biophysical and behavioral sciences

11. The FIRST element of the nursing process is
    A. planning   B. evaluating
    C. diagnosing   D. assessing

12. Which of the following is NOT a functional category of nursing specialty?
    A. Clinical practice   B. Management
    C. Locale   D. Research

13. Nursing goals are written
    A. using qualitative terms for measurement
    B. as both short-term and long-term
    C. for segmented populations of patients
    D. in technical terms

14. State board of nursing activities include each of the following EXCEPT
    A. identifying standards of care
    B. participating in disciplinary actions involving nurses
    C. lobbying for federal legislation involving the scope of nursing
    D. approving schools, curriculum, and the entry requirements into nursing practice

15. Which of the following, if committed by a nurse, is an example of an unintentional tort?
    A. Invasion of privacy   B. False imprisonment
    C. Fraud   D. Malpractice

16. The granting of a legal permit by a government agency to an individual to engage in the practice of nursing is
    A. licensing   B. registration
    C. credentialing   D. certification

17. The knowledge of nurses' accepted professional standards of conduct is known broadly as nursing

   A. ethics B. mores C. norms D. esthetics

18. A licensed practical nurse (LPN) is required by law to practice under the supervision of any of the following EXCEPT a(n)

   A. dentist
   B. registered nurse
   C. homeopathic practitioner
   D. osteopathic physician

19. Which of the following is an organization of both individuals and agencies?

   A. International Council of Nurses (ICN)
   B. American Nursing Association (ANA)
   C. National Federation of Licensed Practical Nurses (NFLPN)
   D. National League for Nursing (NLN)

20. The purpose of the Smith-Hughes Act was to

   A. provide DRG groupings for Medicaid decision-making
   B. establish a Patient's Bill of Rights
   C. establish federal standards for the content of nursing education programs
   D. provide federal funding for vocationally oriented practical nursing programs

21. Which of the following is NOT a trend influencing current nursing practice options?

   A. Increasing emphasis on wellness programs
   B. Greater emphasis on collaborative practice among health professionals
   C. Overall narrowing of practice options
   D. Movement toward community and home health care

22. Which of the following statements about the thinking behind the nursing process is FALSE?
   It

   A. integrates priority setting and feedback mechanisms into every step
   B. involves images rather than verbal symbols (words)
   C. is cyclic and recurring
   D. can be learned in terms of skill and speed

23. The role of a nurse that is prominently expressed when protecting the patient's human rights is that of

   A. manager   B. patient advocate
   C. rehabilitator   D. caregiver

24. Each of the following is a result of Supreme Court rulings on abortion EXCEPT

   A. it is not legally permissible for the state to restrict abortions during the first trimester of pregnancy in any way
   B. the first trimester of pregnancy is defined as the first 3 months of the pregnancy

C. during the second trimester of pregnancy, the mother's privacy rights must yield to reasonable restrictions designed to protect the health and safety of the mother
D. the state has the right to prohibit abortion during the third trimester of pregnancy

25. The protection of nurses' professional capacity and legal control of nursing practice through licensing is generally provided by 25._____

   A. the ANA
   B. nurse practice acts
   C. the American Medical Association
   D. the Smith-Hughes Act

KEY (CORRECT ANSWERS)

1.	C	11.	D
2.	A	12.	C
3.	B	13.	B
4.	C	14.	C
5.	D	15.	D
6.	A	16.	A
7.	B	17.	A
8.	C	18.	C
9.	B	19.	D
10.	B	20.	D

21. C
22. B
23. B
24. A
25. B

TEST 3

DIRECTIONS: Each question or incomplete statement is followed by several suggested answers or completions. Select the one that BEST answers the question or completes the statement. *PRINT THE LETTER OF THE CORRECT ANSWER IN THE SPACE AT THE RIGHT.*

1. Which of the following modes of nursing care evolved from concepts of scientific management developed within the business community?

    A. Team nursing
    B. The case method
    C. The functional method
    D. Primary nursing

2. Which of the following was one of the first to develop a transcultural theory of nursing care?

    A. Nightingale
    B. Watson
    C. Leininger
    D. Peplau

3. Currently, the nursing process method emphasizes

    A. diagnosing
    B. assessing
    C. evaluating
    D. planning

4. The health care consumer's increased awareness of preventive medicine has resulted in an increase in

    A. the number of inpatient admissions
    B. knowledge and services to promote health and prevent illness
    C. anxiety over diagnostic workups such as colonoscopies
    D. the length of hospitalization stays

5. Each of the following legal concepts is implicit in a nurse's role as a provider of service EXCEPT

    A. confidentiality
    B. liability
    C. contractual obligations
    D. standards of care

6. A general duty nurse has been asked by a patient to increase the dosage of a tranquilizer above the prescribed order. The nurse does not comply, because he adheres to the accepted code of conduct and set of norms that he has developed over the years, which is referred to as his

    A. principles of beneficence
    B. value system
    C. advocacy
    D. code of ethics

7. In order to practice as a nurse specialist, one must achieve at least a(n) _____ degree in nursing.

    A. associate
    B. baccalaureate
    C. master's
    D. doctoral

8. Under the prospective payment system of Medicare, reimbursement is made according to

A. financial need
B. the institution's established critical pathways
C. demographics
D. DRG classification system

9. When collecting data during the nursing process, a primary source of data would be

   A. the nurse's observations
   B. other health care providers
   C. data from family and friends of the patient
   D. the patient herself

10. The fact that a nurse's conduct is the hospital's responsibility is an example of the legal doctrine of

    A. caveat emptor
    B. teleology
    C. respondeat superior
    D. stare decisis

11. In 1949, the

    A. National Federation of Licensed Practical Nurses (NFLPN) was founded by Lilian Kuster
    B. U.S. Department of Education commissioned an intensive study to differentiate tasks of practical nurses
    C. National League for Nursing established a Department of Practical Nursing
    D. Household Nursing Association School of Attendant Nursing was founded in Boston

12. A nurse inherently knows that it is morally wrong to strike a patient. This is an example of

    A. teleology
    B. the ethic of caring
    C. intuitionism
    D. deontology

13. Nursing's conceptual model gives clear and explicit direction to each of the following areas of nursing EXCEPT

    A. practice
    B. professional growth
    C. research
    D. education

14. Identifying interventions and alternatives is an element of the _____ phase of the nursing process.

    A. planning
    B. assessing
    C. diagnosing
    D. evaluating

15. The body of law that deals with relationships between individuals and the government is _____ law.

    A. civil   B. private   C. tort   D. public

16. Which of the following is NOT an expressed purpose served by a nurse's professional accountability?
    To

    A. allow the evaluation of new professional practices
    B. prevent costly litigation

C. maintain standards of health care
D. provide a basis for ethical decision-making

17. One of the purposes of the Omnibus Budget Reconciliation Act (OBRA) was to

   A. form a review board responsible for auditing the billing services of physicians' offices
   B. place a larger portion of financial responsibility for health care services on consumers who could afford it
   C. bring a measure of quality assurance to the nursing home industry
   D. establish standards for the documentation of care

18. What is the term for the process of change in which a person's cognitive processes are sufficiently matured so that he or she can solve problems that could not be solved previously?

   A. Accommodation
   B. Revelation
   C. Actualization
   D. Reconciliation

19. Which of the following is NOT a typical research function for a nurse with a master's degree in nursing?

   A. Analyzing and reformulating nursing practice problems so that scientific knowledge and methods can be used to find solutions
   B. Developing methods to monitor the quality of the practice of nursing in a clinical setting
   C. Conducting investigations for the purpose of monitoring the quality of the practice of nursing in a clinical setting
   D. Enhancing the quality and clinical relevance of nursing research by providing expertise in clinical problems

20. Before a civil trial, out-of-court sworn statements, known as _____, are taken by parties and witnesses.

   A. discoveries
   B. depositions
   C. affidavits
   D. interrogatories

21. Each of the following is an advantage associated with the use of critical pathways in health care EXCEPT they

   A. are outcome-driven
   B. result in a more even distribution of health services
   C. provide a time-line to achieve their goals
   D. encourage collaboration by health care workers

22. A student nurse, realizing she has administered the wrong dose of medication to a patient, immediately informs her nurse educator. This student nurse is described ethically as

   A. accountable
   B. penitent
   C. trustworthy
   D. honest

23. Which of the following nursing theories was introduced earliest in nursing history? 23._____

    A. The adaptation model
    B. Self-care theory
    C. The interactive model
    D. The four conservation principles of nursing

24. The growth of professionalism in nursing can be viewed in relation to each of the following EXCEPT 24._____

    A. specialized education
    B. autonomy
    C. organizational affiliation
    D. ethics

25. In a hospital, two nurses discuss the incompetence of a patient's physician. The patient overhears the discussion. 25._____
    The nurses could be held liable for

    A. negligence   B. slander
    C. invasion of privacy   D. libel

KEY (CORRECT ANSWERS)

1. C	11. A
2. C	12. C
3. A	13. B
4. B	14. A
5. A	15. D
6. B	16. B
7. C	17. C
8. D	18. A
9. D	19. B
10. C	20. B

21. B
22. A
23. C
24. C
25. B

TEST 4

DIRECTIONS: Each question or incomplete statement is followed by several suggested answers or completions. Select the one that BEST answers the question or completes the statement. *PRINT THE LETTER OF THE CORRECT ANSWER IN THE SPACE AT THE RIGHT.*

1. In the twentieth century, nursing's professional status has been most clearly advanced by

    A. increased demand for nurses
    B. nursing programs shifting from hospital to university affiliation
    C. increased technical knowledge required for practice
    D. wartime nursing service

2. For a profession or occupation to obtain the right to license its members, it must generally meet each of the following criteria EXCEPT

    A. practice in the profession requires a level of education typically beyond a baccalaureate degree
    B. there is a need to protect the public's safety and welfare
    C. there is a proper authority to assume the obligations of the licensing process
    D. the occupation is clearly delineated as a separate, distinct area of work

3. Once a nurse is actively licensed in one state, licensure in another state is available through the process of

    A. board application and certification
    B. attrition
    C. credentialing
    D. endorsement

4. The first school for practical nurses established in the United States was the

    A. Shepard-Gill School of Practical Nursing
    B. Ballard School
    C. Boston Training School
    D. Thompson Practical Nursing School

5. Which of the following is a characteristic of a career?

    A. Possible intermittent retraining
    B. Evaluation primarily by peers
    C. Work selects person
    D. Variable initial training

6. _____ errors is NOT a general category of nursing care errors that can result in negligence.

    A. Assessment   B. Intervention
    C. Duty   D. Planning

7. Each of the following is a significant reason for the sizable increase in health care costs in recent decades EXCEPT

A. the system of payment for hospitals and physicians
B. inflation
C. general decline in overall health of population
D. increased utilization of health services

8. A nurse who demonstrates organizational ability but lacks a certain speed and flexibility would most likely be professionally categorized as

   A. a novice
   B. an advanced beginner
   C. competent
   D. proficient

9. In what year were the first state nursing licensure laws passed?

   A. 1860   B. 1873   C. 1903   D. 1911

10. Which of the following modes of nursing care delivery is considered to be the precursor to primary nursing?

    A. Team nursing
    B. The case method
    C. The functional method
    D. Community nursing

11. Which of the following is NOT true of informed consent?

    A. It must be given by an individual with the capacity and competence to understand.
    B. The client must be able to complete his or her signature.
    C. The client must be given enough information to be the ultimate decision maker.
    D. It must be given voluntarily.

12. An accredited nursing program

    A. is a federally funded health care program that educates practical nursing students
    B. is necessary before the graduate is eligible to take the National Council Licensing Examination for Practical Nursing (NCLEX-PN)
    C. is one that meets the minimal standards set by the respective state agencies responsible for overseeing educational programs
    D. voluntarily seeks a review by a given organization to determine if the program meets established criteria

13. _____ is a type of diagnostic intervention.

    A. Planning
    B. Monitoring
    C. Referring
    D. D, Meeting basic needs

14. As a concept involved in the health care delivery system, health promotion was slow to evolve until the

    A. 1960s   B. 1970s   C. 1980s   D. 1990s

15. As a client advocate, a nurse's first step in informing a client of a situation and the rights inherent in the situation is to

    A. present information in a way that is meaningful to the client
    B. make sure the information can be accessed
    C. make sure the client agrees to receive the information
    D. deal with those who may not want the client to be informed

16. _____ nursing research is also known as descriptive theory.

    A. Nonexperimental
    B. Experimental
    C. Qualitative
    D. Historical

17. Which of the following is a CURRENT characteristic of nursing practice?

    A. Subservience to the discipline of medicine
    B. Acceptance of ideal nursing care for each patient as an appropriate goal
    C. Hands-on care and psychomotor tasks as the major domain
    D. Rewards occurring through advancement of nursing knowledge

18. Patient-related factors such as attitudes, beliefs, and traits that may be affecting a patient's behavior, but whose effects cannot be validated, are classified as _____ stimuli.

    A. focal
    B. contextual
    C. residual
    D. secondary

19. In 1988, Medicare coverage was expanded to include each of the following EXCEPT

    A. expensive drugs
    B. permanently disabled workers and their dependents eligible for disability insurance under Social Security
    C. catastrophic care
    D. extremely expensive hospital care

20. Which of the following elements of the nursing process is performed LAST?

    A. Diagnosing
    B. Evaluating
    C. Assessing
    D. Implementing

21. The cost of financing health care services is becoming increasingly severe in the United States. Which of the following is NOT a reason for this?

    A. Greater out-of-pocket expense to the consumer
    B. Increased cost of equipment, energy, and labor
    C. Changes in supply and demand
    D. Increased use of highly specialized and technical services

22. Which of the following was identified by the ANA's Commission on Nursing Research as nursing research's most important priority?

    A. Developing cost-efficient delivery systems of nursing care
    B. Decreasing the negative impact of health problems on coping abilities, productivity, and satisfaction
    C. Promoting health and preventing illness
    D. Developing strategies that provide effective nursing care to high-risk groups

23. The first nursing theorist to focus on nursing as an interactive process between nurse and patient was

    A. King   B. Orem   C. Roy   D. Peplau

24. The primary purpose of nursing theory is to

    A. give clear and explicit direction to the aspects of professional practice
    B. generate knowledge in the field
    C. shoe the features of the discipline
    D. integrate concepts into a meaningful configuration

25. The law serves each of the following functions in nursing EXCEPT

    A. help establish the boundaries of independent nursing action
    B. assist in maintaining a standard of nursing practice by making nurses accountable
    C. to outline the major ethical considerations of the profession
    D. differentiate the nurse's responsibilities from those of other health professionals

KEY (CORRECT ANSWERS)

1.	B	11.	B
2.	A	12.	C
3.	D	13.	B
4.	B	14.	C
5.	B	15.	C
6.	C	16.	A
7.	C	17.	D
8.	C	18.	C
9.	C	19.	B
10.	B	20.	B

21.	A
22.	C
23.	D
24.	B
25.	C

EXAMINATION SECTION
TEST 1

DIRECTIONS: Each question or incomplete statement is followed by several suggested answers or completions. Select the one that BEST answers the question or completes the statement. *PRINT THE LETTER OF THE CORRECT ANSWER IN THE SPACE AT THE RIGHT.*

1. A nurse has reached a level of professionalism categorized as *proficient* when he or she
   A. consciously and deliberately plans nursing care and coordinates complex care demands
   B. recognizes a client's readiness to learn how to manage a treatment program
   C. no longer relies on rules or guidelines
   D. perceives a situation as a whole, rather than just its individual aspects

2. A nurse's separate but interdependent legal roles are generally defined as each of the following EXCEPT
   A. provider of service
   B. citizen
   C. guardian
   D. employee or contractor for service

3. Administrative law is written within the scope of the authority granted by the
   A. long-term care facility
   B. hospital
   C. legislative body
   D. school of nursing

4. In 1992, the American Organization of Nursing Executives published its recommendations for effective health care reform in the United States. Which of the following was NOT an element of these recommendations?
   A. Finance health care through an increasing reliance on public-sector funding
   B. Increase health care access by the use of physician and non-physician providers
   C. Make provisions for catastrophic care, with some limitation on extraordinary procedures
   D. Encourage consumer partnerships

5. What is the term for the ongoing process of behaving in ways that lead to improved health, or a subjective perception of balance, harmony, and vitality?
   A. Yin
   B. Wellness
   C. Soundness
   D. Fitness

6. The *adaptive* model of nursing was developed by
   A. Watson
   B. Roy
   C. Parse
   D. Nightingale

7. The voluntary practice of establishing that an individual nurse has met his/her minimum standards of nursing competence in specialized areas is known as
   A. licensing
   B. registration
   C. credentialing
   D. certification

8. According to Peplau, the first phase to develop in a nurse-patient relationship is

   A. resolution
   B. identification
   C. orientation
   D. exploitation

9. The purpose of a nurse's professional code of ethics is, in its most general sense, to

   A. provide standards of conduct for the practice of nursing
   B. provide a tool for interpretation of individual expectations
   C. clearly govern the practice of nursing
   D. state the specific decision-making steps in an ethical dilemma

10. A rehabilitation process typically has each of the following broad objectives EXCEPT to

    A. assist the client to use his or her abilities
    B. return affected abilities to the highest possible level of function
    C. strengthen existing abilities in order to compensate for the loss of others
    D. prevent further disability

11. Persons who perform emergency care in a reasonable and prudent manner, without appropriate equipment and supplies, are protected from legal action in most states by

    A. common law
    B. Good Samaritan laws
    C. liability insurance
    D. nursing practice acts

12. The central concept of _____ is improving or maintaining the quality of life, rather than saving life or curing illness.

    A. the health maintenance organization (HMO)
    B. an independent practice association
    C. hospice services
    D. rehabilitation services

13. The purpose of conscience clauses in state abortion legislation is to

    A. allow medical professionals to refuse participation in third-trimester abortions only
    B. grant hospitals the right to deny admission to abortion clients
    C. implement the federal *gag rule* in hospitals or counseling services about the mention of abortion as an available option
    D. permit nurses or other medical staff to inform patients of their moral obligation to certain procedures

14. Each of the following is true of intentional torts EXCEPT

    A. the act in question is willful and deliberate
    B. the wrong results from failure to use due care
    C. they involve the commission of a prohibited act
    D. they involve certain specific types of conduct listed as *wrong*

15. In which of the following states would a nursing program use the term *vocational nursing* instead of *practical nursing*?

    A. California
    B. New York
    C. Illinois
    D. Hawaii

16. Which of the following modes of nursing care was developed in response to the shortage of personnel experienced in World War II?

    A. Team nursing
    B. The case method
    C. The functional method
    D. Primary nursing

17. Most jurisdictions in the United States have statutes that impose a duty on health care professionals to report certain confidential information. Which of the following is NOT a type of information generally included in these statutes?

    A. Vital statistics
    B. Child or elder abuse
    C. Requested medication
    D. Violent incidents

18. In most states, advanced directives

    A. must be witnessed by at least one person
    B. must be witnessed by two people but do not require review by attorney
    C. may be challenged by members of the client's family
    D. must under all circumstances be reviewed by an attorney

19. The changing nature of the American health care system has involved many implications for nursing practice. Which of the following is NOT one of these?

    A. Greater demand for assessment and evaluation skills
    B. Demand for researching the cost of nursing care in relation to DRG categories
    C. Greater ability to adapt to a more corporate structure
    D. Decreased need for nurses to function in primary care

20. Nursing interventions that are based on the instructions or written orders of another professional are classified as

    A. dependent
    B. interdependent
    C. released
    D. independent

21. A _____ can, under certain circumstances, provide informed consent.

    A. minor
    B. person who is unconscious
    C. client who is sedated and disoriented
    D. mentally ill person who has been judged to be incompetent

22. Which of the following organizations receives and manages funds and trusts that contribute to the advancement of nursing?

    A. International Council of Nurses (ICN)
    B. American Nursing Association (ANA)
    C. National Federation of Licensed Practical Nurses (NFLPN)
    D. National League for Nursing (NLN)

23. Which of the following is NOT an example of a primary health care service?

    A. Illness prevention programs
    B. Referring clients to specialists
    C. Restoring clients to useful function in some or all areas of their lives
    D. Explaining a client's overall health problem

24. A health care professional's duty to do no harm is known as the principle of 24.____

   A. nonmaleficence
   B. autonomy
   C. beneficence
   D. justice

25. The legal term for touching another's body without consent is 25.____

   A. assault
   B. molestation
   C. battery
   D. malicious wounding

KEY (CORRECT ANSWERS)

1.	D	11.	B
2.	C	12.	C
3.	C	13.	B
4.	A	14.	B
5.	B	15.	A
6.	B	16.	C
7.	D	17.	C
8.	C	18.	B
9.	A	19.	D
10.	C	20.	A

21. A
22. A
23. C
24. A
25. C

TEST 2

DIRECTIONS: Each question or incomplete statement is followed by several suggested answers or completions. Select the one that BEST answers the question or completes the statement. *PRINT THE LETTER OF THE CORRECT ANSWER IN THE SPACE AT THE RIGHT.*

1. The MAIN difference between a Preferred Provider Organization (PPO) and a Preferred Provider Arrangement (PPA) involves 1.____

    A. prepaid premiums
    B. whether services are offered to the insurer at a discounted rate
    C. the degree to which a copayment is applied to services
    D. whether a contract is made with individual providers or an organization of providers

2. The term for a mental image or classification of things and events in terms of similarities is 2.____

    A. framework   B. concept   C. model   D. theory

3. Which of the following is NOT a type of advanced medical directive? 3.____

    A. Durable power of attorney
    B. Living will
    C. Power of executor
    D. Health care proxy

4. A patient has signed a consent for a perineal surgical procedure. Consent will be most clearly indicated by the patient's statement that 4.____

    A. he understands but does not know exactly what will be done during the procedure
    B. his wife wants him to go through with the procedure
    C. he understands the stoma may be permanent
    D. he is in so much pain, he'll sign anything

5. By the end of the nineteenth century, there were three nursing schools established in the United States. Which of the following was NOT one of these? 5.____

    A. Connecticut Training School
    B. Bellevue Hospital School of Nursing
    C. Johns Hopkins School of Nursing
    D. Boston Training School

6. Nursing _____ is the term for the way in which nursing knowledge is expressed by a practitioner. 6.____

    A. ethics   B. science   C. theory   D. esthetics

7. The time period of a civil litigation procedure is LEAST likely to be affected by 7.____

    A. whether an injury or death is involved
    B. the attorneys for both sides
    C. the severity of the complaint
    D. the backlog of cases pending before the court

111

8. Which of the following is a characteristic that most clearly distinguishes a profession from other kinds of occupations?

    A. A code of ethics
    B. A complex, sophisticated research apparatus devoted to the enlargement of the body of knowledge pertinent to the role to be performed
    C. The esteem with which members of a society's general population regard the occupation
    D. Its requirement of prolonged specialized training to acquire a body of knowledge pertinent to the role to be performed

9. _____ is covered under Medicare.

    A. Dentures
    B. Examinations to prescribe eyeglasses
    C. Examinations to prescribe and fit hearing aids
    D. Dental care

10. The giving of nursing care is an element of the _____ phase of the nursing process.

    A. implementing   B. assessing
    C. diagnosing   D. evaluating

11. Of the following, the first to offer a definition of *nursing process* was

    A. King   B. Travelbee   C. Abdellah   D. Henderson

12. What type of nursing research has proven to be most difficult to carry out in hospital settings?

    A. Nonexperimental   B. Experimental
    C. Qualitative   D. Historical

13. Each of the following is a general approach to moral theory involved in medical practice EXCEPT

    A. teleology   B. bioethics
    C. intuitionism   D. deontology

14. _____ is a system in which one nurse is responsible for total care of a number of clients 24 hours a day, seven days a week.

    A. Team nursing   B. Case-method
    C. Functional-method   D. Primary nursing

15. The purpose of the prospective payment system (PPS) legislation passed by the federal government in 1983 was *primarily* to

    A. create diagnostic categories for reimbursement
    B. limit the amount of money paid to hospitals that are reimbursed by Medicare
    C. fix the amount of coinsurance for Medicare clients
    D. establish a means of determining reimbursements to providers

16. When performing aggregation, a nurse's FIRST step is to

    A. establish relationships
    B. conduct nursing research

C. collect and summarize clinical interventions
D. develop nursing theory

17. The most common malpractice situations involved in nursing care are   17.____

    A. not giving proper attention to patient complaints
    B. medication errors
    C. client falls
    D. mistaken identity

18. A patient's health records are   18.____

    A. owned by the patient, who always has a right to see them
    B. confidential information that can never be taken to court
    C. concise legal records of all care given and responses
    D. not used by anyone but direct care providers

19. Each of the following is a service or agency that has been added to some hospitals as a result of the changing nature of the health care delivery system EXCEPT   19.____

    A. hospice services   B. nutrition classes
    C. elderly day care   D. fitness classes

20. An LPN is working as a staff member at a nursing home. One of the patients, Mr. Thompson, a 90-year-old, is restless and has spent the last few nights wandering about, unable to sleep. The LPN is told in report by Ms. Barkley, a fellow nurse, that Ms. Barkley borrowed a Darvocet from another patient and gave it to Mr. Thompson to calm him down. After the LPN discusses the problem with Ms. Barkley and reports the error to the physician, the next appropriate action would be to   20.____

    A. call her attorney to file a complaint
    B. bring the issue to the organization's ethics committee
    C. report the problem to the State Department of Health
    D. do nothing, since an oral reprimand was given

21. The regulation of nursing is a function of   21.____

    A. the ICN   B. the ANA
    C. state law   D. federal law

22. In order to resolve ethical dilemmas, a nursing staff should establish a sound database that will address each of the following questions EXCEPT: 22.____

    A. What is the patient's religious affiliation?
    B. What is the intent of the proposed action?
    C. What persons are involved in the situation?
    D. What are the possible consequences of the proposed action?

23. In 1914,   23.____

    A. the Thompson Practical Nursing School was founded in Brattleboro, Vermont
    B. the association of Practical Nursing Schools was founded

C. the Mississippi State Legislature was the first political body to pass license laws controlling practical nurses
D. Galen Health Institutes, Inc. opened practical/ vocational nursing programs in several states

24. When collecting data during the nursing process, a tertiary source of data would be

    A. the patient himself
    B. the patient's record
    C. data from family and friends of the patient
    D. the nurse's observations

25. Which of the following is an example of public law affecting nurses?

    A. Sexual assault
    B. Americans with Disabilities Act
    C. Malpractice
    D. Living wills

24.____

25.____

KEY (CORRECT ANSWERS)

1.	D	11.	A
2.	B	12.	B
3.	C	13.	B
4.	C	14.	D
5.	C	15.	B
6.	D	16.	C
7.	B	17.	B
8.	D	18.	C
9.	B	19.	A
10.	A	20.	B

21. C
22. A
23. C
24. B
25. A

TEST 3

DIRECTIONS: Each question or incomplete statement is followed by several suggested answers or completions. Select the one that BEST answers the question or completes the statement. *PRINT THE LETTER OF THE CORRECT ANSWER IN THE SPACE AT THE RIGHT.*

1. The CHIEF goal of a nurse in the role of care provider is to

    A. execute planned nursing interventions
    B. convey understanding of about what is important, and to provide support
    C. help the client to recognize and cope with stressful psychological or social problems
    D. prevent illness

    1.____

2. Each of the following is characteristic of the process for developing critical pathways in a medical care facility EXCEPT

    A. a consensus is developed around the management of the case type by a multidisciplinary team that includes physicians
    B. information used includes insurance reimbursements
    C. before it becomes policy, a pathway is piloted in a clinical setting
    D. the process for developing a pathway is created independent of the agency

    2.____

3. For legal purposes, the standards of care for nursing practice are most clearly defined by the

    A. NLN's Standards of Care
    B. ICN's Code of Ethics
    C. ANA's Code for Nurses
    D. state nurse practice act

    3.____

4. Which of the following is a typical research function of a nurse at the associate degree level?

    A. Using nursing practice as a means of gathering data to refine and extend practice
    B. Reading, interpreting, and evaluating research for applicability to nursing practice
    C. Sharing research findings with colleagues
    D. Assisting in data collection within an established, structured format

    4.____

5. According to the International Council of Nurses, the nurse's fundamental ethical responsibilities include the following EXCEPT to

    A. prevent illness
    B. sustain a cooperative relationship
    C. restore health
    D. alleviate suffering

    5.____

6. A nurse who demonstrates marginally accepted performance is professionally categorized as

    A. a novice   B. an advanced beginner
    C. competent   D. proficient

    6.____

115

7. A resident physician instructs nurses to order a complete blood count and urinalysis on all clients admitted to the emergency room and to get the results before calling him down. The nurses feel this is unethical; it is wasteful and causes discomfort and possible risks for the clients. Without having the authority to change the situation, however, they order the tests, feel guilty, and upset. This is an example of

    A. a decision-focused ethical problem
    B. an action-focused ethical problem
    C. intuitionism
    D. a deontological ethical problem

8. Each of the following has contributed to the professional nurse's increased role as a teacher EXCEPT

    A. new emphasis on health promotion
    B. increased client awareness
    C. shortened hospital stays
    D. increase in long-term illnesses and disabilities

9. According to Miller, the critical aspects of professionalism in nursing do NOT include

    A. delineating and specifying the skills and competencies that are the boundaries of expertise
    B. attaining a competence derived from the theoretical base
    C. gaining a body of knowledge in a university setting
    D. gaining a science orientation at the hospital level in nursing

10. When the American Society of Superintendents of Training Schools of Nursing was established in 1894, its primary goal was

    A. to promote the establishment of nursing education programs throughout the United States
    B. the increase in prestige and remuneration of civil nursing practice as compared to wartime nursing
    C. the establishment of educational standards for nursing
    D. recruitment and training of qualified nursing personnel

11. The general term for an expected standard of behavior for specific group members is

    A. folkway   B. law   C. rule   D. norm

12. It is NOT a purpose of nursing codes of ethics to

    A. give direction for actions to take in specific cases
    B. remind nurses of the special responsibility they assume when caring for the sick
    C. provide a sign of the profession's commitment to the public it serves
    D. guide the profession in self-regulation

13. _____ stimuli are most immediate to a patient, and precipitate certain observed behaviors.

    A. Focal   B. Contextual
    C. Residual   D. Primary

14. Since 1965, health care costs in the United States have increased by approximately

    A. 100%   B. 200%   C. 400%   D. 600%

15. Before a civil trial, written answers to written questions, known as _____, are submitted by all parties.

    A. discoveries
    C. affidavits
    B. depositions
    D. interrogatories

16. In what year were the Medicare amendments to the Social Security Act adopted?

    A. 1945   B. 1955   C. 1965   D. 1975

17. Which of the following is a type of therapeutic intervention?

    A. Educating
    C. Inspecting
    B. Monitoring
    D. Observing

18. Which of the following is NOT typically involved in a nurse's responsibility as witness to a client's informed consent?

    A. Witnessing the client's signature
    B. Witnessing the exchange between the client and the physician
    C. Establishing that the client fully understands
    D. Securing the approval of a patient's living relation

19. Of the following, which patient value is most threatened by health care situations?

    A. Equity   B. Security   C. Autonomy   D. Well-being

20. Which of the following is a secondary health care agency?

    A. Hospice
    C. Long-term care facility
    B. Crisis center
    D. Hospital

21. Which of the following is NOT an important priority of data collection during the assessment phase of the nursing process?

    A. Communicating with the client, rather than consulting secondary sources
    B. Including information about both strengths and needs
    C. Arranging results in a way easily retrievable by future researchers
    D. Including the client's responses to current alterations

22. Which of the following was the creator of nursing's *four conservation principles*?

    A. Neuman   B. Orem   C. Levine   D. Rogers

23. Which of the following is not an essential element of nursing diagnosis?

    A. Focusing on person's responses
    B. Labeling conclusions
    C. Suggesting interventions
    D. Representing an opinion

24. Each of the following is a recommendation offered by the ANA regarding *do not resuscitate* (DNR) orders EXCEPT

    A. the wishes of the client's spouse and family must always take precedence
    B. when the client is incompetent, an advance directive or the surrogate decision-makers should make treatment decisions
    C. if it is contrary to the nurse's personal beliefs to carry out a DNR order, the nurse should consult the nursing manager for a change in assignment
    D. a DNR order is separate from other aspects of a client's care, and does not imply that other types of care should be withdrawn

25. The scientific method is useful in nursing research for

    A. applying research principles into real-world practice
    B. overcoming current inabilities to measure most concepts of interest to nurses
    C. to find answers to clinical problems
    D. helping to answer ethical or value questions

KEY (CORRECT ANSWERS)

1. B		11. D	
2. D		12. A	
3. D		13. A	
4. D		14. C	
5. B		15. D	
6. B		16. C	
7. B		17. A	
8. B		18. D	
9. D		19. C	
10. C		20. D	

21. C
22. C
23. D
24. A
25. C

EXAMINATION SECTION
TEST 1

DIRECTIONS: Each question or incomplete statement is followed by several suggested answers or completions. Select the one that BEST answers the question or completes the statement. *PRINT THE LETTER OF THE CORRECT ANSWER IN THE SPACE AT THE RIGHT.*

1. Which of the following is NOT a goal associated with the use of critical pathways in medical care.
   To

   A. promote professional and collaborative practice and care
   B. establish standards of practice for health care professionals
   C. achieve realistic, expected client and family outcomes
   D. reduce costs and the length of stay

   1.____

2. The organization largely responsible for the voluntary accreditation of nursing education programs in the United States is the

   A. National League for Nursing (NLN)
   B. International Council of Nurses (ICN)
   C. Joint Commission on Accreditation of Healthcare Organizations (JCAHO)
   D. American Nurses Association (ANA)

   2.____

3. Which of the following is NOT generally considered to be a goal of the contemporary health care system?

   A. Return of autonomy and independence to the client
   B. Return of health care professionals to more generalized education and practice
   C. Increased emphasis on preventive care
   D. Acceptance of good health as a responsibility of the client, care provider, and society

   3.____

4. Nurses who want to ensure their autonomy in the workplace generally seek

   A. administrative positions
   B. research positions
   C. expanded clinical competence
   D. private practice

   4.____

5. Each of the following was a feature of Florence Nightingale's original nursing program at St. Thomas Hospital EXCEPT that

   A. the program was financially linked to the hospital
   B. the training lasted 1 year
   C. records were kept on student and graduate progress for the purpose of establishing standards
   D. training included both formal instruction and practical experience

   5.____

6. The earliest mode of nursing care in use was

   A. team nursing
   B. the case method
   C. the functional method
   D. primary nursing

   6.____

7. The body of law that defines and enforces duties and rights among private individuals that are not based on contractual agreements is _____ law.

   A. criminal   B. private   C. tort   D. public

8. According to Miller, the degree to which a nurse functions as a professional is reflected in each of the following behaviors EXCEPT

   A. assessing, planning, implementing, and evaluating theory
   B. preserving and promoting the professional organization as the major referent
   C. accepting, promoting, and maintaining the independence of nursing research from nursing practice
   D. upholding the service orientation of nursing in the public eye

9. If a nurse is inequitably assigned to a shift or weekend work, the category of collective bargaining that has been breached is

   A. violations of federal or state law
   B. contract violations
   C. management responsibilities
   D. violation of agency rules

10. Immediately after World War II, the United States experienced a dire shortage of civilian nurses. The primary reason for this was

    A. a lack of clear nursing education standards for nursing education and practice
    B. low pay and poor working conditions for civilian nurses as opposed to nurses in military service
    C. growth and diversity became a major emphasis in the health care industry
    D. a marked increase in the civilian population

11. In the United States, the system of law rests on four basic principles. Which of the following is NOT one of these?

    A. Each individual has rights and responsibilities.
    B. Law is characterized by change.
    C. Law is based on a concern for the distribution of material wealth and the opportunity to acquire it.
    D. Actions are judged on the basis of a universal standard of what a similarly educated, reasonable, and prudent person would have done under similar circumstances.

12. As a general rule, professional codes of ethics are

    A. typically more demanding than legal standards
    B. used as a framework for legislation
    C. composed in order to protect members of the profession from legal action
    D. formulated in order to conform to legal standards

13. The _____ approach to nursing research is also known as the literary or critical approach.

    A. nonexperimental   B. experimental
    C. qualitative   D. historical

14. Which of the following promoted the facilitation of the *body's reparative processes* by manipulating a patient's environment?

    A. Rogers
    B. Maslow
    C. Levine
    D. Nightingale

15. If a nurse makes a documentation error while charting a patient, the nurse should _____, write *error in charting* above the incorrect section, and initial the changes.

    A. cross out the error with a single line
    B. *white out* the error
    C. in a differently colored ink, draw an enclosure around the error
    D. skip a line

16. The ANA recommends that each of the following questions be part of the nursing admission assessment regarding advanced directives EXCEPT:

    A. Is the client preparing for a procedure for which an advance care directive might be applicable?
    B. Does the client wish to initiate an advance care directive?
    C. Does the client have basic information about advanced directives?
    D. If the client has prepared an advance care directive, did the client bring it to the health care agency?

17. The amount of autonomy a professional group possesses depends *primarily* on its effectiveness at

    A. governing its members
    B. delineating a professional code of ethics
    C. securing rights for its members
    D. providing legal protection for its members

18. The hospice movement in the United States gathered most of its momentum in the

    A. 1950s   B. 1960s   C. 1970s   D. 1980s

19. Analysis is a feature of the _____ phase of the nursing process.

    A. planning
    B. assessing
    C. diagnosing
    D. evaluating

20. When documenting care and observations in a patient record,

    A. approved medical terms and abbreviations can be used
    B. black or dark blue ink should be used
    C. abbreviation should be avoided at all times to avoid errors
    D. locally adopted abbreviations can be used

21. Which of the following is LEAST likely to factor in nurses' ethical decision-making?

    A. The professional code ethics
    B. Moral principles
    C. Legal principles
    D. Nurses' perception of roles and responsibilities

22. In order to protect themselves legally, nurses must question each of the following types of orders from physicians EXCEPT

    A. those that differ in any way from those conventionally encountered in similar situations
    B. those given after a client's condition has changed
    C. those that a client questions
    D. standing orders

23. The professional organization for nurses in the United States is the

    A. International Council of Nurses (ICN)
    B. American Nursing Association (ANA)
    C. National Federation of Licensed Practical Nurses (NFLPN)
    D. National League for Nursing (NLN)

24. Which of the following is an example of a secondary health care service?

    A. Preventive care
    B. Advanced specialized diagnostic care
    C. Referral to specialists
    D. Surgery

25. Today, the most significant effect of advances in technology and knowledge in the health care industry has been to

    A. improve diagnostic procedures
    B. change the profile of the hospital client
    C. increase the specialization of professionals
    D. make more effective drugs available to clients

KEY (CORRECT ANSWERS)

1. B		11. C	
2. A		12. A	
3. B		13. D	
4. A		14. D	
5. A		15. A	
6. B		16. A	
7. C		17. A	
8. C		18. C	
9. B		19. C	
10. B		20. A	

21. C
22. A
23. B
24. D
25. B

TEST 2

DIRECTIONS: Each question or incomplete statement is followed by several suggested answers or completions. Select the one that BEST answers the question or completes the statement. *PRINT THE LETTER OF THE CORRECT ANSWER IN TEE SPACE AT THE RIGHT.*

1. Each of the following is a category used to define different clinical specialties for nursing EXCEPT   1._____

    A. illnesses
    B. age groups
    C. locales
    D. teaching

2. In 1945,   2._____

    A. the National League for Nursing established a Department of Practical Nursing
    B. New York became the only state to have mandatory licensure laws for practical nurses
    C. the Smith-Hughes Act was passed
    D. the association of Practical Nursing Schools was founded

3. A nurse becomes _____ by the process of learning the ways of the nursing culture, and becoming a functioning participant in this group.   3._____

    A. proficient
    B. socialized
    C. autonomous
    D. professional

4. Each of the following is a burden of proof required for nursing negligence and malpractice EXCEPT a(n)   4._____

    A. injury to the client
    B. duty of the nurse to the client
    C. causal relationship between the nurse's breach of duty and the subsequent injury to the client
    D. willful breach of the nurse's duty to the client

5. Which of the following is a typical research function of a nurse at the baccalaureate level?   5._____

    A. Assisting others to apply scientific knowledge in nursing practice
    B. Conducting investigations for the purpose of monitoring the quality of practice of nursing in a clinical setting
    C. Identifying nursing problems that need to be investigated and participates in the implementation of specific studies
    D. Developing methods for scientific inquiry of phenomena relevant to nursing

6. Which of the following is NOT a typical characteristic of an Independent Practice Association (IPA)?   6._____

    A. Clients pay a fixed prospective payment to the IPA.
    B. Care is provided in physicians' offices.
    C. At the end of a fiscal year, any surplus money is divided among the provider and the IPA.
    D. The IPA pays the provider directly.

7. Nursing _____ includes knowledge obtained through nursing research.

   A. ethics   B. science   C. theory   D. esthetics

8. Which of the following is an example of constitutional law affecting nurses?

   A. Living wills
   B. Nurse and employer contracts
   C. Sexual harassment laws
   D. Due process

9. Of the following, which moral framework is based on relationships, rather than on the concept of justice?

   A. Teleology
   B. The ethic of caring
   C. Intuitionism
   D. Bioethics

10. A *novice* is a nurse

    A. who can demonstrate marginally accepted performance
    B. who enters a clinical setting with no experience
    C. who has not yet begun nursing education
    D. whose practice is essentially flexible

11. Each of the following is a basic rule for a nurse to follow in charting a patient EXCEPT

    A. mark each block of a charting or entry with one's initials
    B. all sheets should contain the patient name, date, and time
    C. use direct quotes when appropriate
    D. use only black ink

12. In what year had all states passed licensure laws affecting practical/vocational nurse training?

    A. 1914   B. 1941   C. 1955   D. 1961

13. The main DISADVANTAGE associated with the functional mode of nursing care delivery is

    A. fragmentation of care
    B. economic inefficiency
    C. high personnel demand
    D. overwhelming emotional involvement with client

14. Which of the following is an example of a major tertiary care provider?

    A. Long-term care facility
    B. Home health care agency
    C. Industrial clinic
    D. Ambulatory care center

15. Which of the following is a characteristic that most clearly distinguishes a profession from other kinds of occupations?

A. An orientation of the individual toward service, either to a community or to an organization
B. The interdependence of individuals for the advancement of the occupation's influence on the greater culture
C. A long history of the occupation's development and change over time
D. Its requirement for involvement of practitioners in a society's greater civic culture

16. Each of the following is a reason why preventive health care facilities have been slow to develop in the United States EXCEPT

   A. consumers have been more aware of treatment of illness than of prevention and health promotion
   B. preventive health costs are not covered by most private insurers
   C. physicians are largely oriented to illness in their practice
   D. the nurse's role as chief provider of preventive health care has been slow to evolve, and the treatment of illness often takes precedence over preventive health care activities

17. When developing a definition of health, one should consider that health is

   A. a condition of physical, mental, and social well-being and absence of disease
   B. a static condition; the absence of pathology
   C. the ability to pursue the activities of daily living
   D. a function of the physiological state

18. In what year was the Patient Self-Determination Act passed by the United States government?

   A. 1965   B. 1973   C. 1980   D. 1991

19. Which of the following is NOT a purpose generally served by nursing ethics committees? To

   A. evaluate institutional experiences related to reviewing decisions having ethical implications
   B. direct educational programs that provide knowledge regarding ethical principles and issues for the medical and professional community
   C. participate in disciplinary actions involving nurses who have proven to be in violation of the agency's code of ethics
   D. assist hospital nursing and medical staff in the development and review of policies related to ethical responsibilities

20. The listing of a nurse's name and other information on an official roster of a governmental or nongovernmental agency is a process known as

   A. licensing   B. registration
   C. credentialing   D. certification

21. As the nursing process method first came into accepted use, most practitioners' attention was focused on

   A. diagnosing   B. assessing
   C. evaluating   D. implementing

22. Which of the following states uses a Title Act, rather than a practice act, to regulate nursing licensure?

    A. Florida   B. Ohio
    C. Texas   D. California

23. The ANA's Human Rights Guideline for Nurses in Clinical and Other Research attempts to specify each of the following EXCEPT the

    A. type of research activities appropriate for nurses at differing educational levels
    B. type of activities involved
    C. mechanisms necessary to ensure that protection is adequate
    D. persons to be safeguarded

24. In 1973, the

    A. Omnibus Budget Reconciliation Act was passed
    B. Health Maintenance Organization Act was passed
    C. Center for Disease Control was established
    D. National Institutes of Health were founded

25. Which of the following is NOT a type of critical pathway variance?

    A. System   B. Treatment   C. Provider   D. Client

KEY (CORRECT ANSWERS

1.	D	11.	A
2.	B	12.	C
3.	B	13.	A
4.	D	14.	B
5.	C	15.	A
6.	C	16.	B
7.	B	17.	A
8.	D	18.	D
9.	B	19.	C
10.	B	20.	B

21. B
22. C
23. A
24. B
25. B

TEST 3

DIRECTIONS: Each question or incomplete statement is followed by several suggested answers or completions. Select the one that BEST answers the question or completes the statement. *PRINT THE LETTER OF THE COERECT ANSWER IN THE SPACE AT THE RIGHT.*

Questions 1-12.

DIRECTIONS: Questions 1 through 12 refer to the list below of several theorists and practitioners who have contributed to the development of nursing as a profession. In the space at the right of each person's main theory of nursing, place the letter that corresponds to the person's name.

A. Levine
B. King
C. Rogers
D. Orem
E. Orlando
F. Henderson
G. Watson
H. Travelbee
I. Leininger
J. Neuman
K. Abdellah
L. Parse

1. The three elements of the nursing situation are patient behavior, nurse reaction, and nurse action. 1.____

2. A nurse's goal is to be kind and caring but also intelligent, competent, and technically well-prepared to provide service to individuals, families, and society. 2.____

3. The goal of nursing is to use conservation activities aimed at optimal use of a patient's resources. 3.____

4. Caring is assisting persons in performing activities they would accomplish independently given the necessary resources. 4.____

5. The goal of nursing is to maintain and promote health, prevent illness, and care for and rehabilitate ill and disabled patients through the *humanistic science of nursing*. 5.____

6. The interpersonal process is viewed as a human-to-human relationship formed during an illness or *experience of suffering*. 6.____

7. The focus of nursing is on humanity as a living unity, and its qualitative participation with health experience. Health is a continual, open process, rather than a state of well-being or an absence of disease. 7.____

8. Nursing is defined as a process of action, reaction, and interaction whereby nurse and client share information about their perceptions in the nursing situation, leading to goal attainment. 8.____

9. The goal of nursing is to provide care consistent with nursing's emerging science and knowledge, with care as the central focus. 9.____

10. Nursing's primary concern is persons and their self-care actions. 10.____

11. Stress reduction is the goal of the systems model of nursing. 11.____

12. Caring is an interpersonal process comprising interventions that result in meeting human needs. 12.____

13. In 1965, the American Nurses Association published a position paper outlining its beliefs about the nursing profession. Which of the following was NOT a belief included in this paper?

    A. The minimum preparation for technical nursing practice should be an associate degree in nursing.
    B. Nursing assistants should have preservice programs in vocational education, rather than on-the-job training.
    C. The minimum preparation for the beginning professional nurse should be baccalaureate degree in nursing.
    D. Nursing education should take place in affiliation with a health care institution, typically a general hospital.

14. Those acts that are permitted to be performed or prohibited from being performed by a prudent person working within the parameters of his/her training, license, and experience, and the conditions existing at the time, are defined broadly as

    A. the Code of Ethics
    B. the nurse practice act
    C. Standard Operating Procedures
    D. Standards of Care

15. Documentation is part of the _____ phases of the nursing process.

    A. assessment   B. planning
    C. implementation   D. evaluation

16. Nursing's first professional code of ethics was adopted in

    A. 1860   B. 1941   C. 1953   D. 1980

17. Mrs. Yardley is a hospital patient with congestive heart failure. She is a bit forgetful and unsteady on her feet. In the past, she has fallen several times, and the nursing staff is concerned for her safety. After some consideration, Mrs. Yardley is provided with a safety reminder device when the nurse cannot be in attendance. The necessary action for Mrs. Yardley's protection interferes, out of necessity, with her ability or tendency to function independently.
    This situation becomes a potential threat to her

    A. nonmaleficence   B. value system
    C. autonomy   D. informed consent

18. The ANA's Patient's Bill of Rights includes each of the following elements EXCEPT

    A. a hospital must ask the client about any advance directive before certain procedures are begun
    B. the client's right to refuse a treatment or particular plan of care
    C. if a client lacks decision-making capacity for any reason, the rights will be exercised on their behalf at the discretion of the physician who is currently treating or caring for the client
    D. confidentiality of all records and communications regarding a client's care

19. A nurse _____ provides bedside or direct care in a specialty area.   19.____

    A. practitioner   B. clinician
    C. generalist   D. specialist

20. Which of the following is an example of statutory law affecting nurses?   20.____

    A. Nurse practice acts   B. Active euthanasia
    C. Negligence   D. Equal protection

21. Which of the following is NOT a type of primary health care agency?   21.____

    A. Industrial clinic   B. Ambulatory care center
    C. Hospital   D. Physician's office

22. A profession is considered to be autonomous if it(s)   22.____

    A. standards are legislated by a federal government
    B. regulates itself and sets standards for its members
    C. is divided into a federation of regionally independent factions
    D. members are affiliated with a national organization

23. A nurse, committed to the sanctity of life, wants a client to have artificial nutrition and   23.____
    hydration. However, the nurse also knows that tube-feedings are prolonging the client's
    pain and suffering, and this makes the nurse want to discontinue the feedings. This is an
    example of

    A. a decision-focused ethical problem
    B. an action-focused ethical problem
    C. intuitionism
    D. moral distress

24. _____ nursing research approach organizes narrative or words to discover themes and   24.____
    relationships among concepts in a non-numerical way.

    A. Nonexperimental   B. Experimental
    C. Qualitative   D. Historical

25. In what year did Florence Nightingale begin the transformation of nursing from occupa-   25.____
    tion to profession by establishing the nursing school at St. Thomas Hospital in London?

    A. 1853   B. 1860   C. 1873   D. 1894

KEY (CORRECT ANSWERS)

1. E
2. K
3. A
4. F
5. C

6. H
7. L
8. B
9. I
10. D

11. J
12. G
13. D
14. D
15. C

16. C
17. C
18. C
19. B
20. A

21. C
22. B
23. A
24. C
25. B

EXAMINATION SECTION
TEST 1

DIRECTIONS: Each question or incomplete statement is followed by several suggested answers or completions. Select the one that BEST answers the question or completes the statement. *PRINT THE LETTER OF THE CORRECT ANSWER IN THE SPACE AT THE RIGHT.*

1. All of the following are generally accepted moral values basic to clinical nursing practice EXCEPT 1.____

    A. nonmaleficence
    B. veracity
    C. countertransference
    D. fidelity

2. Values clarification is a process by which individuals find their own answers (values) to situations. 2.____
   Valuing is composed of seven processes, that can be placed in which of the following groups?

    A. Prizing one's beliefs and behaviors
    B. Choosing one's beliefs and behaviors
    C. Acting on one's beliefs
    D. All of the above

3. Behavior must be consistent over a period of time in order to reflect a value. 3.____
   It is important for nurses to do all of the following EXCEPT

    A. examine their own values and clarify them
    B. confront the patient with their values
    C. recognize the differences in the values of peers, other health care professionals, and health care organizations
    D. recognize the differences in the values of patients and accept them

4. Which of the following is NOT an advantage of values clarification? 4.____

    A. It serves as a guide for assessing patient's values and provides direction for nursing interventions.
    B. It gives insight into the source of a particular value.
    C. It fosters the making of choices.
    D. It sets limits on the type of nursing activities that can be undertaken.

5. Values change from time to time as situations change. Reasons for identifying a patient's value system do not include 5.____

    A. helping a patient discover a new and meaningful value system following injury or illness
    B. helping the patient explore alternative goals and intervention strategies when valued goals cannot be realized
    C. controlling patient behaviors through value manipulation
    D. planning nursing interventions that support the patient's cultural and health care beliefs

6. All of the following are means of learning a patient's values EXCEPT 6.____

131

A. conversation with a patient about job, family, pets, hobbies, goals or material possessions
B. trying to adopt an authoritative role in patient's thought process
C. listening to patient's family and friends
D. reviewing patient's health records revealing personal values

7. Different patients exhibit different behaviors. Behaviors that may indicate unclear values include all of the following EXCEPT

   A. ignoring a health professional's advice
   B. prior history of cooperation and consistent behavior
   C. inconsistent communication or behavior
   D. confusion or uncertainty about which course of action to take

8. An ethical or moral dilemma is a situation involving a choice between equally satisfactory or unsatisfactory alternatives or a difficult problem that seems to have no satisfactory solution.
   According to Thompson and Thompson, for a situation to be a moral dilemma, it MUST fulfill which of the following criteria?

   A. Awareness of different options
   B. Personal nature of the dilemma
   C. A lack of acceptable alternatives
   D. All of the above

9. Nursing codes of ethics

   A. provide a means by which professional standards of practice are established, maintained, and improved
   B. give the members of the profession a set of guidelines for negotiating contracts
   C. limit the type of work a nurse can ethically attempt
   D. all of the above

10. Purposes of ethical nursing codes include all of the following EXCEPT

    A. providing a basis for regulating the relationship between the nurse, patient, coworker, society, and the profession
    B. serving as a basis for professional curricula and for orienting the new graduate to professional nursing practice
    C. providing a standard basis for including the unscrupulous nursing practitioner and for defending a practitioner who is correctly accused
    D. assisting the public in understanding professional nursing conduct

11. All of the following statements agree with the American Nurses Association Code for nurses EXCEPT:

    A. The patient's right to privacy is safeguarded by judiciously protecting information of a confidential nature
    B. Nurses do not assume responsibility and accountability for individual nursing judgments and actions
    C. Nurses maintain competence in nursing care
    D. Nurses participate in the profession's efforts to implement and improve standards of nursing

12. In addressing the issue of risk versus responsibility to patients, the American Nurses Association presents fundamental criteria to differentiate the nurse's moral duty from the moral option to care for a patient, namely whether

    A. the patient is at significant risk of harm, loss or damage if the nurse does not assist
    B. the nurse's intervention or care is directly relevant to preventing harm
    C. the benefit the patient will gain outweighs any harm the nurse might incur and does not present more than minimal risks to the health care provider
    D. all of the above

13. All of the following statements about the Canadian Nurses Association Code of Ethics for nursing are correct EXCEPT the nurse

    A. is not obliged to hold confidential all information regarding a patient learned in the health care setting
    B. has an obligation to be guided by consideration for the dignity of patients
    C. is obligated to provide competent care to patients
    D. is obligated to represent the ethics of nursing before colleagues and others

14. The withdrawal of equipment from a patient whose life is being sustained by artificial means is a highly complex issue.
    The Hastings Center has prepared guidelines for the termination of life-sustaining treatment, which are governed by all of the following values EXCEPT

    A. the patient's well-being
    B. the nurse's autonomy
    C. integrity of the health professional
    D. justice or equity

15. Although codes of ethics offer general guidelines for decision-making, more specific guidelines are necessary in many cases to resolve the ethical dilemmas encountered by nurses in practice settings.
    Suggested guidelines for nurses to resolve these dilemmas include

    A. establishing a sound data base
    B. disregarding any conflicts presented by the situation
    C. establishing a single course of action in advance
    D. all of the above

16. Nurses need to gather as much information as possible about a situation.
    Aroskar suggests that nurses get answers to all of the following EXCEPT what

    A. persons are involved and what is their involvement in the situation
    B. diagnostic workup the nurse has to perform for a particular case
    C. is the proposed action and what is the intention of the proposed action
    D. are the possible consequences of the proposed action

17. Nursing practice is governed by many legal concepts. Knowledge of laws that regulate and affect nursing practice are needed to

    I. ensure that the nurse's decisions and actions are consistent with current legal principles
    II. protect the nurse from liability
    III. protect the patient
    IV. protect the hospital

The CORRECT answer is:

D. I only   E. II, III   F. I, II   G. I, III, IV

18. Functions of law in nursing do NOT include

    A. providing a framework for establishing which nursing actions in the care of patients are legal
    B. differentiating the nurse's responsibilities from those of the other health professionals
    C. protecting nurses from culpability for their errors
    D. all of the above

19. The Constitutions of the United States and Canada include due process and equal protection clauses. The due process clause applies to state or provincial and local agencies, including public hospitals, and to actions that deprive a person of life, liberty or property. This includes which of the following primary elements?

    A. The rules being applied must be reasonable.
    B. Fair procedures must be followed when enforcing the rules.
    C. The rules being applied must not be vague.
    D. All of the above

20. Laws govern the relationships of private individuals with the government and with each other.
    All of the following are types of law EXCEPT

    A. contact   B. tort
    C. contract   D. constitutional

21. Our system of law rests upon all of the following principles EXCEPT:

    A. Law is based on a concern for justice and fairness
    B. Law is characterized by resistance to change
    C. Actions are judged on the basis of a universal standard of what a similarly educated, reasonable and prudent person would have done under similar circumstances
    D. Each individual has rights and responsibilities

22. Licenses are legal permits granted by a government agency for the practice of a profession and the use of a particular title.
    In order for a profession or occupation to need or hold a license, its members must GENERALLY meet which of the following criteria?

    A. There is little need to protect the public's safety or welfare.
    B. The occupation is clearly delineated as a separate and distinct area of work.
    C. There is no organization suitable in ability to assume the obligations of the licensing process.
    D. All of the above

23. The ANA has enumerated the principles of credentialing. These principles reflect the belief that credentialing exists PRIMARILY to protect and benefit the public and includes   23.____

    A. accountability as an essential component of any credentialing process
    B. professional identity and responsibility evolving from the credentialing process
    C. an effective system of role delineation
    D. all of the above

24. In the United States, nurses are issued a license by the State Board of Nursing or by an administrative governmental agency.   24.____
    Licenses are issued to all of the following registered nurses EXCEPT nurses who have

    A. successfully completed a course of study in a school of nursing accredited by State Board
    B. completed three years of basic training in a private or government hospital
    C. passed the National Qualifying Examinations with a score that is acceptable to the Board
    D. paid the required fees

25. There are two types of licensure/registration: mandatory and permissive.   25.____
    Under mandatory licensure, all nursing practice must be licensed EXCEPT practice

    A. in an emergency
    B. by nursing students as part of their education
    C. by nurses employed by the federal government
    D. all of the above

KEY (CORRECT ANSWERS)

1.	C	11.	B
2.	D	12.	D
3.	B	13.	A
4.	D	14.	B
5.	C	15.	A
6.	B	16.	B
7.	B	17.	C
8.	A	18.	C
9.	A	19.	D
10.	C	20.	A

21. B
22. B
23. D
24. B
25. D

TEST 2

DIRECTIONS: Each question or incomplete statement is followed by several suggested answers or completions. Select the one that BEST answers the question or completes the statement. *PRINT THE LETTER OF THE CORRECT ANSWER IN THE SPACE AT THE RIGHT.*

1. A contract is an agreement between two or more competent persons, upon sufficient consideration, to do or not to do some lawful act.
Contract law requires all of the following elements be met in order to make a contract valid EXCEPT

   A. the act contracted for must be legal
   B. there must be no compensation for the service to be provided
   C. there must be mutual agreement about the services to be contracted for
   D. the parties to be contracted must be of legal age and competent to enter a binding agreement

1.___

2. Nurses have three separate, interdependent legal roles, each with its own rights and associated responsibilities. These roles include

   A. provider of service
   B. employee or contractor for service
   C. citizen
   D. all of the above

2.___

3. While working in the capacity of employee or contractor for service, a nurse has all of the following legal rights EXCEPT the right to

   A. adequate and qualified assistance as necessary
   B. adequate working conditions, e.g., safe equipment and facilities
   C. compensation for services rendered
   D. reasonable and prudent conduct by other health care givers

3.___

4. Most jurisdictions of the country have statutes that impose a duty to report certain confidential information. Major reporting categories include all of the following EXCEPT

   A. vital statistics, e.g., births and deaths
   B. infections and communicable diseases
   C. cancer and other serious conditions
   D. child or elder abuse

4.___

5. A tort is a civil wrong committed against a person or a person's property.
All of the following statements are unintentional torts EXCEPT

   A. they can result from either an act of commission or an act of omission
   B. the act in question is willful and deliberate
   C. the wrong results from failure to use due care
   D. they are not spelled out in an all-inclusive list

5.___

6. Obtaining informed consent is the responsibility of a physician.
The nurse's responsibility is often to witness the giving of informed consent and involves

6.___

A. witnessing the exchange between the patient and the physician
B. notarizing the patient's signature
C. determining that the patient really did understand
D. all of the above

7. Northrop describes major elements of informed consent as including all of the following EXCEPT that

   A. the consent must be given voluntarily
   B. the consent must be given by an individual with the capacity and competence to understand
   C. in order to give consent, the patient must feel coerced
   D. the patient must be given enough information to be the ultimate decision maker

7.____

8. The American Heart Association has issued standards and guidelines for cardiopulmonary resuscitation and emergency cardiac care, outlining the medicolegal considerations and offering recommendations about DNR orders for physicians. The implications of the American Heart Association code standards means that a nurse must do all of the following EXCEPT

   A. ensure that the DNR order is written on the patient's order sheet and progress notes
   B. if the physician refuses to write a DNR order, follow agency policies and procedures
   C. even if the agency does not have a well-established procedure, do not seek a legal opinion
   D. if none of the above steps provide the nurse with sufficient guidelines, the nurse must make a personal decision based on moral values and sense of humanity

8.____

9. Clinical guidelines for the legal precautions that a nurse should adopt include

   A. observe and monitor the patient accurately
   B. build and maintain good rapport with patients
   C. protect patients from falls and preventable injuries
   D. all of the above

9.____

10. Abortion laws provide specific guidelines for nurses about what is legally permissible. The results of Supreme Court rulings do NOT include which of the following statements?

    A. It is not legally permissible for the state to restrict or regulate abortions during the first trimester of pregnancy, except to require that abortions be performed by licensed physicians.
    B. During the second trimester of pregnancy, the mother's privacy rights override any restrictions designed to protect the health and safety of the mother.
    C. During the third trimester of pregnancy, the state has the right to prohibit abortion.
    D. All of the above

10.____

11. Nurses are expected to know basic information about procedures and medications ordered by a physician. Becker outlines all of the following orders that nurses must question in order to protect themselves legally EXCEPT to question

11.____

A. any order a patient questions
B. standing orders, especially if the nurse is inexperienced
C. verbal orders to avoid miscommunication
D. any order if the patient's condition remains the same

12. Nursing students are responsible for their actions and are liable for their acts of negligence committed during the course of clinical experience.
In order to fulfill their responsibilities to patients and to minimize chances for liability, nursing students need to do all of the following EXCEPT

    A. make sure they are prepared to carry out the necessary care for assigned patients
    B. not ask for additional help or supervision
    C. comply with the policies of the agency in which they obtain their clinical experience
    D. comply with the policies and definitions of responsibility supplied by the school of nursing

12.____

13. A will is a declaration by a person about how the person's property is to be disposed of after death.
In order for a will to be valid, which of the following conditions must be met?

    A. The person making the will must be of sound mind.
    B. The person must not be influenced in any way by anyone else.
    C. The person must be physically healthy.
    D. All of the above

13.____

14. In the past, health care facilities have been influenced largely by the needs of the people providing the services. As a result, preventive health care facilities have been slow to develop.
This delay can be attributed in great part to the fact that

    A. physicians are largely oriented toward preventing illness in their practice
    B. consumers have been less aware of treatment of illness then of prevention and health promotion
    C. the nurse's role as the chief provider of preventive health care and health promotion has been slow to evolve
    D. all of the above

14.____

15. The health delivery system is very much affected by a country's total economic status.
Correct statements about economic influences include all of the following EXCEPT:

    A. Inflation and the economic recession of the early 1980's brought increasing concern about escalating health care costs
    B. Medical care costs have increased more than 400% since 1965
    C. The United States spends $1 billion a day on health care and costs are still rising
    D. The United States spends more on health care than it does on defense

15.____

16. Funding for personal health care can come from a variety of sources.
Major sources include all of the following EXCEPT

    A. governments (social insurance)
    B. individual clients
    C. private organizations
    D. health insurance

16.____

17. Primary care agencies are the point of entry into the health care system and the point at which initial health care is given.
    The major purpose of primary care centers is to provide all of the following EXCEPT

    A. long term and chronic care
    B. treatment of permanent malfunctioning that does not require hospitalization
    C. emergency care
    D. health maintenance

    17.____

18. Ambulatory care centers are being used more frequently in many communities. These centers have all of the following advantages EXCEPT they

    A. permit patients to live in a controlled environment while obtaining needed health care
    B. provide medical, nursing, laboratory, and radiologic services
    C. free costly hospital beds for seriously ill patients
    D. all of the above

    18.____

19. An HMO is a group health care agency that provides basic and supplemental health maintenance and treatment services to voluntary enrollees.
    To be federally qualified, an HMO company must meet certain requirements which include offering all of the following EXCEPT

    A. physician's services
    B. short-term mental health services
    C. preventive dental services for children over 12 years of age
    D. laboratory and radiological services

    19.____

20. The preferred provider organization (PPO) has emerged as another alternative health delivery system.
    Major sponsors of PPOs include all of the following EXCEPT

    A. individual patients   B. hospitals
    C. physicians   D. insurance companies

    20.____

21. In 1987, the Congress of the United States passed the Omnibus Budget Reconciliation Act (OBRA) to bring a measure of quality assurance to the nursing home industry. One of the provisions of OBRA that concerns nursing is the requirement for nursing aide training.
    Specific requirements include

    A. a training program of 50 hours for nurse's aides
    B. a registry for nurse's aides
    C. a training program of 25 hours for nurse's aides already providing care
    D. all of the above

    21.____

22. Nursing implications of this 1987 OBRA provision include

    A. concerns about which state agency is to be responsible for implementing the requirements
    B. that the training requirements may not be sufficient to prepare aides to carry out routine care for nursing home patients who have complex problems
    C. the evaluation requirement necessitates job analysis and the development of standard criteria at the state level
    D. all of the above

    22.____

23. The American Hospital Association published *A Patient's Bill of Rights* in an effort to promote the rights of hospitalized clients.
The nursing implications of the patient's bill of rights are that the patient has the right to

    A. considerate and respectful care
    B. refuse treatment to the extent permitted by law
    C. expect reasonable continuity of care
    D. all of the above

24. The problem of financing health illness services is increasingly severe.
Major reasons for increased costs include all of the following EXCEPT

    A. existing equipment and facilities are continually becoming obsolete as research discovers new and better methods
    B. the relative number of people who provide health illness services has decreased
    C. the total population has grown and the demands for services has increased
    D. inflation increases all costs

25. The number of homeless people in towns and cities continues to grow.
Reasons for this increase include all of the following EXCEPT

    A. an increase in federal subsidies for low-income housing
    B. alcohol and drug abuse
    C. deinstitutionalization of mental health facilities and a change in laws governing commitment of the mentally ill
    D. the rising cost of housing

KEY (CORRECT ANSWERS)

1.	B		11.	D
2.	D		12.	B
3.	A		13.	A
4.	C		14.	C
5.	B		15.	D
6.	A		16.	C
7.	C		17.	B
8.	C		18.	A
9.	D		19.	C
10.	B		20.	A

21. B
22. D
23. D
24. B
25. A

EXAMINATION SECTION
TEST 1

DIRECTIONS: Each question or incomplete statement is followed by several suggested answers or completions. Select the one that BEST answers the question or completes the statement. *PRINT THE LETTER OF THE CORRECT ANSWER IN THE SPACE AT THE RIGHT.*

1. The official accrediting body for programs in nursing is the   1.____

    A. National League for Nursing (NLN)
    B. American Medical Association (AMA)
    C. United Nursing League (UNL)
    D. American Nurses' Association (ANA)

2. The MINIMUM formal education that would be required for the position of Assistant Director of Nursing, Intensive Care Unit, is normally   2.____

    A. A.D.
    B. B.S.N.
    C. M.S.
    D. M.S.N. with two years' related experience

3. Which of the following is NOT a typical legal liability affecting nursing practice?   3.____

    A. Forgery
    B. Malpractice
    C. Larceny
    D. Battery

4. Each of the following is considered to be an advantage associated with associate nursing degree programs EXCEPT   4.____

    A. available to part-time students
    B. preparation for administrative roles
    C. relatively diverse student population
    D. efficient use of time

5. Which of the following would be considered grounds for false imprisonment charges to be filed against a nurse?   5.____

    A. Threatening to strike a patient
    B. Failing to protect a patient from injury
    C. Restraining a patient
    D. Performing blood tests on a patient without the patient's consent

6. The National Council Licensure Examination, or NCLEX, examines a candidate's knowledge of client needs along each of the following dimensions EXCEPT   6.____

    A. physical integrity
    B. effective care environment
    C. effective treatment plan
    D. health promotion/maintenance

7. All of the following may be used as reasons for revoking a nursing license EXCEPT

   A. emotional problems
   B. drug addiction
   C. acts that endanger the public
   D. incompetence

8. What is the term used to designate the curriculum track followed by students in a baccalaureate program who have received their basic education through an AD or diploma program?

   A. Elective B. Matriculated
   C. Articulated D. Core

9. What is the MINIMUM formal education that would usually be required for the position of Oncology Nursing Coordinator?

   A. A.D.
   B. B.S.N.
   C. M.A.
   D. M.P.H., with B.S. in nursing

10. R.N.s who return to school for a B.S.N. or M.S.N. degree should consider all of the following factors EXCEPT

    A. prior knowledge and patterns of thought
    B. differences in age and lifestyle
    C. present ability to supervise and evaluate
    D. acquired socializations

11. Formal recognition of a nurse's demonstration of competency by professional organizations or institutions (and not by state or federal boards) is termed

    A. credentialing B. certification
    C. licensure D. accreditation

12. Professional nursing practice requires, as a minimum level of education, a(n)

    A. associate degree B. nursing diploma
    C. baccalaureate degree D. master's degree

13. What is the MINIMUM formal education that would be required for the position of Nursing Instructor, Associate Degree Program?

    A. A.D.
    B. B.S.N.
    C. M.S. in psychiatric or medical-surgical nursing
    D. Any M.S.N. with two years' work experience

14. Candidates who plan to take either the SAT or ACT should register AT LEAST _____ in advance.

    A. six months B. three months
    C. six weeks D. three weeks

15. For purposes of litigation, standard of care is determined by all of the following EXCEPT   15.____

    A. specialty care associations
    B. emergency room statistics
    C. manuals
    D. agency policies

16. Which of the following is NOT a designation given by the American Nurses' Association?   16.____

    A. R.N., C.   B. R.N., C.S.
    C. C, R.N., C.N.A.A.   D. R.N., F.A.A.N.

17. Of the following, an ADVANTAGE associated with nursing diploma programs is   17.____

    A. accelerated level of patient contact
    B. that it offers transfer-level nursing courses
    C. qualification for most non-hospital positions
    D. diverse student population

18. What is the MINIMUM formal education that would usually be required for the position of Clinical Specialist?   18.____

    A. A.D.
    B. B.S.N.
    C. M.S. in field of specialty
    D. M.S.N. with two years' related experience in field of specialty

19. In choosing a nursing school, it is desirable to select a program affiliated with hospitals that have been approved by the   19.____

    A. NLN   B. AMA   C. AHA   D. JCAHO

20. The legal concept describing commonly accepted measures of competence and action on the part of medical professionals is termed   20.____

    A. nursing process
    B. standard of care
    C. interdependent intervention
    D. baseline competency

21. What is the MINIMUM formal education that would usually be required for the position of Clinical Nursing Coordinator?   21.____

    A. B.S.N.
    B. B.S.N. with five years' related clinical experience
    C. M.A.
    D. M.S.N.

22. The legal term for failure to act in a thoughtful manner, which results in harm to another, is   22.____

    A. defamation   B. assault
    C. malpractice   D. negligence

23. In which of the following organizations is membership composed of both nurses and non-nurses?

   A. ANA   B. AANA   C. AORN   D. NLN

24. Each of the following is an advantage associated with baccalaureate nursing programs EXCEPT

   A. preparation for leadership roles in community health
   B. broad general education requirements
   C. lower relative cost
   D. demanding curriculum

25. In order to avoid litigation, verbal or telephone orders from a physician should be signed within _____ hours.

   A. 10   B. 18   C. 24   D. 48

KEY (CORRECT ANSWERS)

1. A		11. B	
2. C		12. C	
3. C		13. C	
4. B		14. C	
5. C		15. B	
6. C		16. D	
7. A		17. A	
8. C		18. C	
9. D		19. D	
10. C		20. B	

21. B
22. D
23. D
24. C
25. C

TEST 2

DIRECTIONS: Each question or incomplete statement is followed by several suggested answers or completions. Select the one that BEST answers the question or completes the statement. *PRINT THE LETTER OF THE CORRECT ANSWER IN THE SPACE AT THE RIGHT.*

1. What is the MINIMUM formal education that would usually be required for the position of Director, School of Nursing (baccalaureate)?

    A. M.S.N.
    B. M.S.N. with five years' experience
    C. M.S.N. with ten years' experience
    D. Ph.D.

2. Of the following terms used in recognizing a nurse's demonstration of competency, _____ is MOST commonly applied in nursing.

    A. credentialing B. certification
    C. licensure   D. accreditation

3. Currently, MOST nurses obtain R.N. status through completion of a(n)

    A. diploma program   B. associate degree
    C. baccalaureate degree D. master's degree

4. Which of the following is NOT one of the fifteen areas of nursing practice that is offered certification by the American Nurses' Association?

    A. Adult nurse practitioner
    B. Clinical specialist in community health nursing
    C. High-risk perinatal nurse
    D. Clinical specialist in child and adolescent psychiatric and mental health nursing

5. A student in a master's program must USUALLY complete _____ units of academic study, in addition to 8 units of graduate professional work.

    A. 18-24   B. 24-30   C. 30-36   D. 36-45

6. The MINIMUM formal education that would usually be required for the position of Director, Home Health Agency, is the

    A. B.S.N.   B. M.S.N.   C. M.P.H.   D. Ph.D.

7. What is the legal term GENERALLY used to describe any form of professional misconduct?

    A. Malpractice   B. Incompetence   C. Negligence   D. Corruption

8. A candidate in an R.N. diploma program will USUALLY take _____ years to complete requirements.

    A. 1-2   B. 2-3   C. 4   D. 4 or more

9. Technical nursing practice requires a(n) _____ as a MINIMUM level of education.

   A. high school diploma
   B. associate degree
   C. baccalaureate degree
   D. master's degree

10. Which of the following mechanisms for controlling the quality of professional practice has NO legal status?

    A. Credentialing
    B. Certification
    C. Licensure
    D. Accreditation

11. A candidate who takes the College Level Examination Program (CLEP) General Examination can eliminate some tuition costs by earning as many as _____ semester hours of undergraduate credit.

    A. 12   B. 24   C. 30   D. 36

12. In legal terms, a written communication that damages a person's reputation is specifically known as

    A. defamation   B. slander   C. assault   D. libel

13. Each of the following is considered to be a disadvantage associated with practical nursing programs EXCEPT

    A. little upward mobility
    B. relative difficulty in qualifying for hospital work
    C. limited working capacity
    D. narrowly specialized education requirements

14. What is the MINIMUM formal education that would be required for the position of Visiting Staff Nurse?

    A. A.D.   B. B.S.N.   C. M.S.   D. M.S.N. or M.P.H.

15. Which of the following types of nursing practice does NOT require completion of either a nursing diploma or an associate degree?

    A. L.P.N.   B. M.S.N.   C. R.N.   D. C.C.R.N.

16. All of the following are considered to be grounds for filing assault and battery charges against a nurse EXCEPT

    A. performing urine tests without the patient's consent
    B. coercing patients into an unwanted treatment
    C. detaining a patient in an institution
    D. moving a protesting patient

17. The MINIMUM formal education that would be required for the position of Head Nurse CCU is

    A. A.D.
    B. B.S.N.
    C. M.S.
    D. M.S.N. with two years' related clinical experience

18. Which of the following is considered to be a disadvantage associated with baccalaureate nursing programs?

    A. Initial cost
    B. Limited qualification for non-hospital positions
    C. Limited student population
    D. Difficulty advancing to graduate study

19. Which of the following mechanisms for controlling the quality of professional practice is implemented through the use of state board examinations and state-approved schools of nursing?

    A. Credentialing
    B. Certification
    C. Licensure
    D. Accreditation

20. For purposes of litigation, the standard of care might be determined by

    A. expert witnesses
    B. NCLEX test scores
    C. institutional statistics
    D. patient testimony

21. From the time a student graduates from a school of nursing until he or she becomes licensed, the nurse works in the capacity of

    A. a licensed practical nurse
    B. a graduate nurse under a state-issued permit
    C. an undergraduate nurse under a limited institutional permit
    D. nurse's assistant

22. Of the following, one of the fifteen areas of nursing practice that is offered certification by the American Nurses' Association is

    A. gynecological nurse practitioner
    B. radiological nurse
    C. family nurse practitioner
    D. gastrointestinal nurse

23. The National Council Licensure Examination, or NCLEX, identifies all of the following as the five main behaviors that make up the nursing process EXCEPT

    A. prescribing
    B. planning
    C. assessing
    D. evaluating

24. The MINIMUM formal education that would be required for the position of Visiting Nurse Clinical Specialist is the

    A. A.D.
    B. B.S.N.
    C. M.S.
    D. M.S.N. with two years' related clinical experience

25. Affirmation that a school of nursing has requested evaluation and successfully met criteria established by the state board of registered nursing is termed

    A. credentialing
    B. certification
    C. licensure
    D. accreditation

KEY (CORRECT ANSWERS)

1. D
2. A
3. B
4. B
5. C

6. C
7. A
8. B
9. B
10. B

11. C
12. D
13. B
14. B
15. A

16. C
17. B
18. A
19. C
20. A

21. B
22. C
23. A
24. C
25. D

EXAMINATION SECTION
TEST 1

DIRECTIONS: Each question or incomplete statement is followed by several suggested answers or completions. Select the one that BEST answers the question or completes the statement. *PRINT THE LETTER OF THE CORRECT ANSWER IN THE SPACE AT THE RIGHT.*

1. Of the following management approaches, expecting _____ would be MOST likely to harm quality improvement initiatives.

    A. a quick fix from quality improvement
    B. CQI to save the organization money
    C. organization-wide involvement in QI
    D. role change throughout the organization

    1._____

2. Setting MINIMUM standards of care would probably lead to an emphasis on

    A. excellence
    B. higher goals
    C. mediocrity
    D. performance below minimum standards

    2._____

3. Quality improvement initiatives should _____ the process or service.

    A. begin the process and be built into
    B. begin the process, but are evaluated only at the end of
    C. end the process and be built into
    D. end the process, but are evaluated only at the end of

    3._____

4. Promotion should be PRIMARILY based on

    A. age   B. education   C. seniority   D. skills

    4._____

5. The Joint Commission views the compartmentalization of services, service activities, and quality improvement activities (i.e., by department) as

    A. the best means of implementation
    B. one of the best means of implementation
    C. a moderately effective means of implementation
    D. a weakness in implementing quality improvement

    5._____

6. A patient will MOST likely rate a health care center highly if he or she perceives that

    A. the physician shows high technical competence
    B. the physical facility is well-maintained
    C. the technology provided is the newest available
    D. physicians and staff show a caring attitude

    6._____

7. The fact that structure leads to process, and process leads to outcome, would best be described as a(n) _____ relationship.

    A. causal   B. comparative
    C. interdependent   D. relational

    7._____

149

8. Monitoring radiographic film quality by technologists addresses which aspect of care?

    A. Administrative
    B. Process
    C. Outcome
    D. Structure

9. Monitoring the time it takes a nurse to perform a procedure would address which aspect of care?

    A. Administrative
    B. Process
    C. Outcome
    D. Structure

10. It is the ultimate responsibility of _____ for communicating quality in an organization.

    A. staff
    B. middle management
    C. physicians
    D. top management

11. *Respondeat superior* in healthcare agencies is typically interpreted as

    A. borrowed servant
    B. corporate liability
    C. *quid pro quo*
    D. *res ipsa loquitor*

12. Removal of the left leg, when the right leg was the diseased part that required removal, would be seen legally as

    A. *non compis*
    B. *quid pro quo*
    C. *res judicata*
    D. *res ipsa loquitor*

13. Grouped healthcare providers competing in a given geographic region would most likely be called

    A. case management
    B. managed care
    C. managed competition
    D. prospective payment

14. The Joint Commission uses the term *important functions* to refer to
    I. key governance and management functions
    II. key clinical and support functions
    III. legal and fiduciary obligations to patients

    The CORRECT answer is:

    A. I, II
    B. I, III
    C. II, III
    D. I, II, III

15. Blood usage review by medical/professional staff must occur at LEAST

    A. weekly
    B. monthly
    C. semi-annually
    D. annually

16. Licensed independent practitioners are granted privileges for periods of no longer than _____ year(s).

    A. one
    B. two
    C. three
    D. five

17. Timely intervention is MOST likely possible with a _____ review system.

    A. concurrent
    B. focused
    C. prospective
    D. retrospective

18. Which of the following would NOT be considered a discrete variable?

    A. Nurses working in the hospital
    B. Hospitals in a system
    C. Patients with HIV
    D. Infection rate

19. A managed care plan is said to have undergone favorable selection when it(s)

    A. members are sicker than the average person in the capitated population
    B. members are healthier than the average person in the capitated population
    C. makes less money than previous years
    D. makes more money than previous years

20. Which standard decides the basis on which a health plan is determined to be financially responsible for a member's unauthorized visit to an emergency department or specialist?

    A. Encounter data
    B. Prudent layperson standard
    C. Severity adjustment
    D. Solvency standard

21. Providers who traditionally serve large numbers of low income and uninsured people are termed

    A. indemnity health plan
    B. provider sponsored organization
    C. point-of-service option
    D. safety net providers

22. What best describes a health plan or insurance network that allows members to receive defined services from non-network providers?

    A. Indemnity health plan
    B. Provider sponsored organization
    C. Point-of-service option
    D. Safety net providers

23. A health plan that allows for self-referral to a specialist without first having obtained a referral is known as

    A. prepaid health plan
    B. provider sponsored organization
    C. open access
    D. point-of-service option

24. Which of the following is NOT true regarding the JCAHO standards on restraints?

    A. Orders may be made by licensed independent practitioners.
    B. Orders must include specific time limits.
    C. Organizational policy must be reflected in medical records.
    D. Surgical and other devices are included.

25. Which of the following are required measurements in hospital quality improvement plans?
    I. Needs, expectations, and satisfaction of patients
    II. Staff views of PI opportunities
    III. Medication use

    The CORRECT answer is:

    A. I, II   B. I, III   C. II, III   D. I, II, III

KEY (CORRECT ANSWERS)

1. A
2. C
3. A
4. D
5. D

6. D
7. A
8. C
9. B
10. D

11. B
12. D
13. C
14. A
15. B

16. B
17. A
18. D
19. B
20. B

21. D
22. C
23. C
24. D
25. D

TEST 2

DIRECTIONS: Each question or incomplete statement is followed by several suggested answers or completions. Select the one that BEST answers the question or completes the statement. *PRINT THE LETTER OF THE CORRECT ANSWER IN THE SPACE AT THE RIGHT.*

1. Which one of the following BEST describes organizational culture and change? 1.____

   A. It is best to move quickly with change.
   B. Professionals are relatively easy to convince of the need for change.
   C. The factor most often misjudged in the change process is the magnitude of change required and the staff response to change.
   D. Ingrained mindsets are incapable of change; thus, they should simply be eliminated from the change process.

2. Which of the following is the MOST common reason for failure of quality improvement initiatives? 2.____

   A. The expectation that managers will become part of the change process
   B. The expectation that staff will become part of the change process
   C. Viewing quality improvement as a long-term process
   D. Viewing quality improvement as a short-term fix

3. The best view of outcomes is that they should be _____ focused. 3.____

   A. patient   B. physician
   C. staff   D. statistically

4. Which of the following is the MOST common mistake in the use of consultants? 4.____

   A. Following their recommendations blindly
   B. Not following their recommendations at all
   C. Hiring based on cost
   D. Not checking the references and track record of the consultant

5. From the standpoint of the hospital, which one of the following best fits all three roles of customer, processor, and supplier? 5.____

   A. CEO   B. Employee   C. Patient   D. Physician

6. The capitation rate paid for a Medicare member is _____% of the adjusted average per capita cost. 6.____

   A. 100   B. 95   C. 75   D. 66

7. Which of the following are considered to be coordinated care plans under Medicare+Choice? 7.____
   I. Health Maintenance Organizations
   II. Preferred Provider Organizations
   III. Provider Sponsored Organizations
   The CORRECT answer is:

   A. I, II   B. I, III   C. II, III   D. I, II, III

8. Which one of the following is NOT true regarding the JCAHO's interpretation of environment of care?

    A. All employees must be determined competent before care is rendered.
    B. Building evacuation is not required during quarterly fire drills.
    C. Physicians are not included in this function.
    D. Waste and utility systems management is a *must know* item.

9. Which of the following is NOT true regarding the JCAHO's *no smoking* policy?

    A. Exceptions to the prohibitions are usually determined by licensed, independent practitioners.
    B. Social rehabilitation settings may not require a licensed independent practitioner's order.
    C. Exceptions are allowed in hospital-sponsored ambulatory care areas.
    D. Exceptions are not allowed in adolescent and child patient care areas.

10. A histogram with a *twin peaks* appearance is also called a(n) _____ distribution.

    A. bimodal
    B. high variability
    C. isolated peak
    D. minimal variability

11. Which of the following is NOT a source of information for the National Practitioner's Data Bank?

    A. American Medical Association
    B. Healthcare entities
    C. Insurance companies
    D. Medical boards

12. A laboratory can receive a waiver from meeting expanded proficiency testing standards under the Clinical Laboratory Improvement Act of 1988 provided

    A. all of its technologists and physicians are appropriately licensed/certified
    B. the lab is in a state-recognized physician's office
    C. the lab is hospital-based
    D. the lab only performs simple tests

13. Which one of the following best describes the intent of OSHA regulations?

    A. The maintenance of hazardous materials
    B. The maintenance of safe, healthful work conditions
    C. The maintenance of medical devices
    D. Conformance to federal labor law

14. Which one of the following is not part of the Patient Self-Determination Act?

    A. Informing requirements for hospitals
    B. Informing requirements for physicians
    C. Durable power of attorney
    D. Living wills

15. Which one of the following is NOT true regarding peer review immunity under the Health-care Quality Improvement Act?

    A. Clinical psychologists are included as possible plaintiffs.
    B. It applies only to hospitals using formal peer review processes.
    C. It does not prevent federal antitrust actions.
    D. It is considered to be a conditional legislation.

16. Rejecting the null hypothesis and concluding that population means are not equal, when they in fact are, is

    A. known as a Type I error
    B. known as a Type II error
    C. less likely if the alpha is set at .05 (as opposed to .01)
    D. less likely if the alpha is set at .10 (as opposed to .05)

17. The National Practitioner Databank was established by the _____ and became operational in _____.

    A. Health Care Quality Improvement Act of 1986; 1986
    B. Health Care Quality Improvement Act of 1986; 1990
    C. Joint Commission; 1986
    D. Joint Commission; 1990

18. Which one of the following is NOT true regarding the National Practitioner Databank?

    A. Health care practitioners may self-query at any time.
    B. Hospitals must query when a practitioner applies for privileges and every two years on practitioners on the medical staff or holding privileges.
    C. Medical malpractice payers may query at any time.
    D. State Licensing Boards may query at any time.

19. Nurse Practice Acts are examples of _____ law.

    A. administrative   B. common
    C. public   D. statutory

20. State Boards of Nursing are examples of _____ law.

    A. administrative   B. common
    C. public   D. statutory

21. Informed consent is not needed when
    I. there is an emergency if there is an immediate threat to life or health
    II. experts agree that it is an emergency
    III. the client is unable to consent and the legally authorized person cannot be reached

    The CORRECT answer is:

    A. I, II   B. I, III   C. II, III   D. I, II, III

22. Which of the following would NOT satisfy the disclosure element of informed consent?

    A. The patient has been informed of current course of medical status and treatment
    B. That the patient has been informed of the risks and benefits of various treatment alternatives
    C. The patient has been told that outcomes can be guaranteed
    D. The patient has been given a professional opinion as to the best alternative

23. Which of the following would constitute voluntary standards used as a guideline for peer review?

    A. ANA Standards of Practice
    B. Credentialing
    C. Licensure
    D. Nurse Practice Acts

24. A person who _____ would NOT be covered under the Americans with Disabilities Act of 1990.

    A. has a communicable disease such as AIDS or HIV
    B. has committed a felony
    C. is recovering from drug or alcohol addiction
    D. is regarded as disabled, whether or not he/she is in fact disabled

25. The error in reasoning made by American business regarding Japanese competition in the 1960s and 1970s was that

    A. no one will buy Japanese products
    B. jobs will never be exported to Japan
    C. Japanese competition is primarily cost competition, not quality competition
    D. statistics are worthless in the business world

KEY (CORRECT ANSWERS)

1.	C	11.	A
2.	D	12.	D
3.	A	13.	B
4.	D	14.	B
5.	C	15.	B
6.	B	16.	A
7.	D	17.	B
8.	C	18.	C
9.	C	19.	D
10.	A	20.	A

21. D
22. C
23. A
24. B
25. C

TEST 3

DIRECTIONS: Each question or incomplete statement is followed by several suggested answers or completions. Select the one that BEST answers the question or completes the statement. *PRINT THE LETTER OF THE CORRECT ANSWER IN THE SPACE AT THE RIGHT.*

1. A manager who _____ best shows leadership in action. 1.____

    A. identifies several new markets for the company based on strategic planning
    B. advocates a *one right way* of doing things
    C. is always pleasant with her employees
    D. is well-viewed in the community

2. To _____ customers is the best delineation of a goal, as it is the least subject to interpretation. 2.____

    A. identify	B. know
    C. appreciate	D. understand

3. In the hospital service delivery process, recent emphasis has been on 3.____

    A. admissions criteria	B. aftercare
    C. continued stay criteria	D. pre-admission processes

4. The composition and qualifications of staff BEST describes staff 4.____

    A. allocation
    B. FTE
    C. mix
    D. roles and responsibilities

5. Which of the following is the best description of the JCAHO's view of model adoption for CQI? 5.____

    A. The ten-step process is a mandatory component.
    B. Outdated models, such as Shewhart's PDCA cycle, should be avoided.
    C. Multiple models are preferred.
    D. The institution must adopt whichever model best fits its needs.

6. JoEllen Smith is determining how many clients still became sick from influenza after receiving flu shots at her facility. Under the JCAHO's Dimensions of Performance, she is evaluating 6.____

    A. appropriateness	B. effectiveness
    C. efficacy	D. safety

7. When JoEllen evaluates how many people in her facility's managed care plan were able to receive the flu shot, she is evaluating, under Dimensions of Performance, 7.____

    A. appropriateness	B. availability
    C. effectiveness	D. efficacy

8. When JoEllen evaluates how many people in her facility's managed care plan were happy with the service received while receiving the flu shot, she is evaluating, under Dimensions of Performance,

   A. effectiveness
   B. efficacy
   C. respect and caring
   D. safety

8._____

9. Robert Smith determines that the laboratory is the cause of the most waiting in his hospital, followed by radiology, and admissions. When he decides to place most of his efforts to decrease wait times by starting with the lab, he is

   A. monitoring quality costs
   B. Pareto planning
   C. rank-ordering
   D. stratifying data

9._____

10. The fewest number of measures in performance monitoring should be in the area of

    A. process
    B. outcome
    C. structure
    D. utilization

10._____

11. An integral part in the process of determining medical necessity in the delivery of quality medical care, including weighing the potential for undesirable outcomes and side effects against the potential for positive outcomes of a treatment best describes

    A. cost-effective medical care
    B. efficacious medical care
    C. efficient medical care
    D. risk-benefit analysis

11._____

12. _____ is correlated to the timeliness of delivered medically necessary standard of care services and supplies which result in the least cost.

    A. Cost-effective medical care
    B. Efficacious medical care
    C. Efficient medical care
    D. Risk-benefit analysis

12._____

13. The selection of the least expensive medically necessary treatment from two or more that are equally efficacious in achieving a desired health care outcome is termed

    A. cost-effective medical care
    B. efficacious medical care
    C. efficient medical care
    D. risk-benefit analysis

13._____

14. Quality improvement and risk management are _____; in the long run, _____ risk translates into _____ quality.

    A. not related; reduced; no change
    B. interrelated; higher; higher
    C. interrelated; reduced; reduced
    D. interrelated; reduced; higher

14._____

15. _____ risk is best described as the risk of doing business.   15.____

    A. Claims   B. Managed care
    C. Marketing   D. Operational

16. Health economic research that focuses on personal satisfaction after retirement would   16.____
    best be described as _____ research.

    A. cost utilization   B. cost minimization
    C. outcomes   D. quality of life

17. Which one of the following is NOT a typical means by which managed care organizations   17.____
    try to reduce costs?

    A. Denial of non-emergency ER visits
    B. Denying all services
    C. Increased use of PAs and NPs
    D. Increased emphasis on prevention and self-care

18. The data shared between institutions to see how each one is doing is BEST defined as   18.____
    _____ data.

    A. comparative   B. definitive
    C. normative   D. relational

19. If a study has 40 true positives and 10 false negatives, then its sensitivity is _____%.   19.____

    A. 8   B. 80   C. 88   D. 90

20. Our Lady Hospital, finding that 80% of its patients are poor over 65 years of age, decides   20.____
    to develop programs specifically for that group. This is called

    A. assessment   B. improvement
    C. reiteration   D. statistical analysis

21. Nancy Smith designs a study to look at two individuals working in the hospital: RNs and 21.____
    CNAs. This is an example of a(n) _____ variable.

    A. acentric   B. causal
    C. dichotomous   D. twin

22. The documentation of basic treatment or action sequence in order to eliminate unneces-   22.____
    sary variation best describes

    A. benchmarking   B. critical path
    C. flow charting   D. variation reduction

23. Under JCAHO's *Cycle for Improving Performance,* historical patterns of performance in   23.____
    the organization is also called

    A. baseline performance
    B. benchmarking
    C. designed performance limits
    D. practice guidelines and parameters

24. The steps involved in JCAHO's *Cycle for Improving Performance* are 24._____
    A. design, measure, assess, and improve
    B. find, organize, clarify, understand, and select
    C. focus, adapt, develop, and evaluate
    D. plan, do, check, and act

25. Which of the following would be the BEST means of charting continuous data? 25._____
    A. Fishbone diagram   B. Flowchart
    C. Histogram   D. Pie chart

KEY (CORRECT ANSWERS)

1. A
2. A
3. B
4. C
5. D

6. C
7. B
8. C
9. C
10. C

11. D
12. C
13. A
14. D
15. D

16. D
17. B
18. D
19. B
20. A

21. C
22. B
23. A
24. A
25. C

TEST 4

DIRECTIONS: Each question or incomplete statement is followed by several suggested answers or completions. Select the one that BEST answers the question or completes the statement. *PRINT THE LETTER OF THE CORRECT ANSWER IN THE SPACE AT THE RIGHT.*

1. (1) Call patient by name; (2) Walk patient back to radiographic room; (3) Perform x-ray exam; is an example of

    A. flowcharting
    B. improvement cycle
    C. planning
    D. process

    1.____

2. Joe Smith wants to study patient satisfaction in his institution, but wants to get the largest group possible so he conducts his study in the local mall. His study might be criticized not only for reaching individuals who are not patients, but also that it is

    A. capitated
    B. nonrandomized
    C. randomized
    D. variated

    2.____

3. Your 6 units receive patient satisfaction scores of 56, 66, 68, 70, 78, 89. What is the mean score for the group?

    A. 56   B. 70   C. 71   D. 89

    3.____

4. Your 6 units receive patient satisfaction scores of 56, 66, 68, 70, 78, 89. Which of the following are accurate representations of range?
    I. 56-89
    II. 33
    III. 71/33
    The CORRECT answer is:

    A. I, II   B. I, III   C. II, III   D. I, II, III

    4.____

5. Death rate as an indicator for the quality of care
    I. often ignores case mix
    II. often ignores regional differences
    III. is the best indicator of physician performance
    The CORRECT answer is:

    A. I, II   B. I, III   C. II, III   D. I, II, III

    5.____

6. Jane Smith develops a patient survey and tests it on a number of patients, who can understand it. She receives fairly identical comments and results. She can consider that this survey meets standards of _____ and _____, but perhaps not _____.

    A. readability; reliability; validity
    B. validity; readability; reliability
    C. reliability; validity; readability
    D. accuracy; validity; readability

    6.____

7. The method of case management with the longest history is _____ case management.

    A. institution based
    B. private based
    C. reimbursement
    D. social welfare

    7.____

161

8. The three displays of a scattergram show   8._____

   A. large relation, small relation, narrow relation
   B. normally distributed, left skewed, right skewed
   C. positive relation, neutral relation, negative relation
   D. skewed relation, normal relation, inter-related

9. An affinity diagram groups   9._____

   A. identical ideas   B. people by skill
   C. people by job   D. related ideas

10. The Process Decision Program Chart (PDPC) is a combination of _____ and _____   10._____
    diagrams.

    A. Fishbone; flow   B. Fishbone; GANTT
    C. Fishbone; tree   D. GANTT; affinity

11. Whereas strategic planning focuses on _____, tactical planning focuses on _____.   11._____

    A. immediate; long range   B. long range; immediate
    C. overview; the process   D. the process; overview

12. If step one in a quality improvement program is to clarify goals, then the next logical step   12._____
    is to

    A. analyze data
    B. educate and build the team
    C. investigate the process
    D. take appropriate actions

13. The best description of a specification is   13._____

    A. measurable aspects of a producer service that match customer needs
    B. specific aspects or attributes of a product or service
    C. written documents
    D. written protocol or policy for action

14. The ideal flow of information in a business or organization is from   14._____

    A. customer to worker to manager
    B. manager to supervisors to workers
    C. manager to workers
    D. vendor to manager to worker

15. Which of the following would most likely NOT represent a typical CQI team?   15._____

    A. Mammographic image quality: radiologist, technologist, physicist
    B. Patient satisfaction: admissions clerk, staff RN, MD, patient representative
    C. Patient transport: transporter, radiology representative, lab representative, staff RN
    D. Product supply: staff technologist, staff RN, medical records clerk

16. The most realistic outcome of Continuous Quality Improvement is an   16._____

    A. improvement may not work, but it is a useful learning tool
    B. improvement will always work if properly carried out

C. improvement will work most of the time but people usually mess them up
D. outcome is a stepping stone to the next higher step

17. Symptomatic treatment is considered inadequate in CQI and performance improvement; instead, the goal must be to

   A. determine the root causes of a problem
   B. find all problems
   C. fix all problems
   D. fix problems at the lowest cost

18. GANTT charts define _____ and _____.

   A. internal processes; external processes
   B. management responsibilities; employee responsibilities
   C. problems; who fixes them
   D. who does what; when

19. In a systems approach, the most important step to avoid frustration and keep working toward future excellence is

   A. converting customer needs to expectations
   B. output or outcomes identification
   C. selection of appropriate measures
   D. the ability to go back to a prior step if a barrier occurs in the process

20. Critical pathways would most likely be developed first for diagnoses and procedures that are high

   A. cost
   B. risk
   C. volume
   D. all of the above

21. Tracking positive variance

   A. tends to show the costlier procedures
   B. tends to show clues to cost-effective care
   C. shows best what doesn't work
   D. helps to track standard practice patterns

22. The need for employees to be seen as autonomous individuals is probably best reflected in

   A. expectancy theory
   B. two-factor theory (Herzberg)
   C. theory X - theory Y
   D. Vroom's preference—expectancy model

23. Which of the following agencies would require age specific criteria for accreditation?
   I. ADA
   II. JCAHO
   III. NCQA
   The CORRECT answer is:

   A. I, II   B. I, III   C. II, III   D. I, II, III

24. When should patients be advised of their rights?
    A. Prior to entry into a healthcare setting
    B. At entry into a healthcare setting
    C. Following entry into a healthcare setting
    D. Patients must ask for explanations of their basic rights

25. The Mammography Quality Standards Act requires direct reporting to patients in which form?
    I. Oral
    II. Written
    III. In lay terms
    The CORRECT answer is:

    A. I, II   B. I, III   C. II, III   D. I, II, III

KEY (CORRECT ANSWERS)

1. D
2. B
3. C
4. A
5. A

6. A
7. D
8. C
9. D
10. C

11. B
12. B
13. A
14. A
15. D

16. A
17. A
18. D
19. D
20. D

21. B
22. D
23. A
24. B
25. A

EXAMINATION SECTION
TEST 1

DIRECTIONS: Each question or incomplete statement is followed by several suggested answers or completions. Select the one that BEST answers the question or completes the statement. *PRINT THE LETTER OF THE CORRECT ANSWER IN THE SPACE AT THE RIGHT.*

1. Which of the following is the BEST reason why the graphic representation of data is usually superior to verbal or written representations?

    A. Faster interpretation
    B. Easier to perform
    C. Most managers can't understand numbers
    D. Easier on the eyes

    1.____

2. Unannounced JCAHO surveys

    A. cannot alter the accreditation status of a hospital
    B. are performed by two specially trained surveyors
    C. are based on five areas identified as problematic based on aggregate data
    D. take three days to perform

    2.____

3. A hospital suddenly realizes that the methods it has been using to plan for the future are illogical and that entirely new methods are needed. This is an example of a

    A. paragon shift   B. paradigm shift
    C. thinking frame   D. thinking shift

    3.____

4. Organizational culture is best defined as

    A. assumptions about individuals and how work gets done
    B. ethnic make-up of employees
    C. provision of activities to employees such as National Nurses Week
    D. professional development of employees

    4.____

5. A good mission statement should include
    I. defining the intent and market of the organization
    II. defining the measure of commitment
    III. ensuring the mission and vision statement are consistent with each other
    The CORRECT answer is:

    A. I, II   B. I, III   C. II, III   D. I, II, III

    5.____

6. The recipient of care is typically best qualified to evaluate which aspect of care?

    A. Availability   B. Continuity
    C. Efficacy   D. Respect and caring

    6.____

7. Which of the following, though important and discussed by the JCAHO, is NOT a joint Commission *Dimension of Performance?*

    A. Availability   B. Competency
    C. Continuity   D. Efficacy

    7.____

165

8. The capacity of any medical test to achieve its desired outcome is known as

   A. appropriateness
   B. continuity
   C. efficacy
   D. effectiveness

9. An HMO that does not fully meet federal criteria for HMOs is called a(n)

   A. autonomous wellness program
   B. competitive medical plan
   C. non-qualified HMO
   D. preferred provider organization

10. What does it mean for a hospital to have a deemed status?

    A. Accredited by HCFA
    B. Denied accreditation by HCFA
    C. Accreditation by an agency recognized by HCFA in lieu of its accreditation survey
    D. Denial of accreditation by an agency recognized by HCFA in lieu of its accreditation survey

11. According to the principles of adult education, which one of the following should the QI Coordinator do first when planning an educational activity?

    A. Assess knowledge and learning needs of learners
    B. Find an appropriate room
    C. Make sure the learning conforms to management's expectations
    D. Determine how the activity will be paid for

12. Which one of the following typically provides the best data regarding continuing education needs of staff?

    A. Case management
    B. Risk management
    C. Quality improvement
    D. Utilization review

13. Which of the following are elements of a well-developed CQI program?
    I. Identify all customers for each service
    II. Development of a CQI panel
    III. Strong, directive management policies
    The CORRECT answer is:

    A. I, II
    B. I, III
    C. II, III
    D. I, II, III

14. Which of the following is the BEST definition of process?

    A. The steps required to provide care
    B. A series of steps that achieve a desired outcome
    C. Patient care activities
    D. Technical aspects of providing care

15. CQI is most likely going to save money by

    A. reducing time spent on training
    B. reducing time spent on meetings
    C. reducing labor and material wastage
    D. all of the above

16. The four foundational elements of the quality improvement process as seen in the Shewhart cycle are

    A. find, organize, clarify, and understand
    B. plan, do, check, and act
    C. find, plan, organize, and do
    D. plan, find, check, and act

17. Hospital A's patient satisfaction score average is 3.6, with a range of scores from 1 to 6. Hospital B has the same score average, but a range of 1 to 5. The standard deviation of Hospital A's scores are MOST likely

    A. high   B. low
    C. moderately effected   D. not effected

18. A hospital wants to look at past patient records to determine trends. This is a _____ study, and involves _____.

    A. retrospective; clinical trials of medications or procedures
    B. retrospective; review of databases and evaluation of patient outcomes
    C. prospective; clinical trials of medications or procedures
    D. prospective; review of databases and evaluation of patient outcomes

19. Who should introduce middle managers to the principles of QI?

    A. QI supervisor   B. Staff
    C. Upper management   D. Outside consultants

20. Which of the following statements BEST reflects the principles of QI?

    A. The team way is the only way.
    B. That is the way we have always done it.
    C. If it isn't broken, don't fix it.
    D. Processes, not employees, are usually to blame.

21. Rhonda Jones thinks that the wait times for outpatients in her facility are excessive, finding her average wait times to be 20 minutes, with a range of 1 minute to 1 hour. Her main benchmarks are 2 local competitors who guarantee wait times of 15 minutes or less. Which of the following is/are logical conclusions, based on the above?

    A. Her wait times are excessive.
    B. Her wait times are acceptable.
    C. She needs more information on how well competitors comply with their guarantee.
    D. None of the above

22. Which of the following graphic representations of data is usually best for showing relationships?

    A. Bar graph   B. Histogram
    C. Pareto chart   D. Scatter diagram

23. Which of the following is typically considered the LEAST restrictive of all health plans?

    A. Capitated payment   B. HMO
    C. Indemnity insurance   D. PPO

24. You have collected trends for the past year showing that 30% of your back injuries happen on the day shift (7-3); 60% on the evening shift (3-11); and 10% on nights (11-7). From a risk management perspective, you should probably begin your back education program on the _____ shift.

    A. day   B. evening   C. night   D. weekend

24.____

25. Which of the following sets contains variables that do not lend themselves to histograms?

    I. Patient waiting times, patient time of day, patient types of exams
    II. Disease population, workload by hour, exam value
    III. Procedure type by hours, computer down time, number of incomplete requests by unit

The CORRECT answer is:

    A. I, II   B. I, III   C. II, III   D. I, II, III

25.____

KEY (CORRECT ANSWERS)

1.	A	11.	A
2.	C	12.	C
3.	B	13.	A
4.	A	14.	B
5.	D	15.	C
6.	D	16.	B
7.	B	17.	A
8.	C	18.	B
9.	B	19.	C
10.	C	20.	D

21. C
22. D
23. C
24. B
25. B

TEST 2

DIRECTIONS: Each question or incomplete statement is followed by several suggested answers or completions. Select the one that BEST answers the question or completes the statement. *PRINT THE LETTER OF THE CORRECT ANSWER IN THE SPACE AT THE RIGHT.*

1. A false positive is when something is

   A. true but the test shows it to be not true
   B. false but the test shows it to be true
   C. true and the test shows it to be true
   D. false and the test shows it to be not true

2. The best differentiation between reliability and accuracy is that reliability has to do with

   A. getting the correct information and accuracy has to do with how often the information is correct
   B. the ability of an instrument to detect and accuracy has to do with how correct that information is
   C. how correct the information is and accuracy has to do with how faithful it is to reality
   D. always getting the same value from the same conditions and accuracy has to do with how correct that value is

3. The LEAST effective time or place to praise an employee for their contribution to a QI team would be

   A. during the annual evaluation
   B. in the employee newsletter
   C. in a staff meeting
   D. on a bulletin board

4. Large purchases tend to come from the _____ budget.

   A. capital   B. equipment
   C. operational   D. incremental

5. If the variation in values between observers is acceptably low, then one has

   A. interobserver reliability
   B. intraobserver reliability
   C. interobserver validity
   D. intraobserver validity

6. Which of the following BEST describes correlation?

   A. Cause and effect
   B. Precursor and event
   C. Events tend to occur at the same time
   D. Events occur independent of each other

7. The most common way of diagramming factors that cause variability in a system is by use of a(n)

    A. line graph
    B. cause & effect diagram
    C. flow chart
    D. affinity diagram

8. What is another name for the Pareto chart?

    A. Bar graph
    B. Scatter graph
    C. Line graph
    D. Flowchart

9. Deming's 14 points can be said to have a(n)

    A. specific managerial structure
    B. emphasis on management by objectives
    C. process orientation
    D. technical emphasis

10. The LEAST important piece of data to know when trending C-section rates by physician is the

    A. number of C-sections
    B. number of deliveries
    C. number of admissions
    D. physician's name

11. You have the opportunity to develop collaborations with neighboring facilities in the sharing of data. Which of the following must be considered first?

    A. Patient confidentiality
    B. Profitability
    C. Economic viability
    D. Technical factors

12. Which of the following are philosophical foundations of CQI?
    I. Systems view
    II. Implementer involvement
    III. Single causation

    The CORRECT answer is:

    A. I, II
    B. I, III
    C. II, III
    D. I, II, III

13. Which of the following would be considered *internal customers* in a hospital?
    I. Physicians
    II. Employees
    III. Patients

    The CORRECT answer is:

    A. I, II
    B. I, III
    C. II, III
    D. I, II, III

14. Which of the following are considered to be customers in a CQI system?
    I. Patient
    II. Provider
    III. Payer

    The CORRECT answer is:

    A. I, II
    B. I, III
    C. II, III
    D. I, II, III

15. When buying software, _____ must be defined first.

    A. the expected outcome
    B. cost considerations
    C. technical considerations
    D. human factors

16. Health care institutions are at risk for which of the following types of utilization?
    I. Over-utilization
    II. Under-utilization
    III. Unexpected utilization
    The CORRECT answer is:

    A. I, II   B. I, III   C. II, III   D. I, II, III

17. The best source for information about quality is the

    A. supplier   B. customer   C. employee   D. manager

18. The function of management in CQI, according to Deming, is to

    A. be responsible for data collection
    B. provide rewards and punishment for performance
    C. track down the causes of poor performance
    D. optimize the system

19. The main reason for failure of a team is

    A. unskilled leadership
    B. lack of effective training
    C. unclear goals, including lack of adequate customer definition
    D. dysfunctional behavior by team members

20. Improving _____ is the primary reason for implementing critical pathways.

    A. financial viability of the institution
    B. physician competency
    C. patient care outcomes
    D. the strategic planning function of an institution

21. Which of the following is the most common interpercentile measure of variability?

    A. Interpercentile measure   B. Normal distribution
    C. Range   D. Standard deviation

22. Which of the following are phases in the formation and use of CQI teams?

    A. Orientation   B. Development
    C. Reiteration   D. All of the above

23. Which of the following would be useful in documenting problems with patient transport?
    I. Flowcharts
    II. Cause-effect diagrams
    III. Pareto charts
    The CORRECT answer is:

    A. I, II   B. I, III   C. II, III   D. I, II, III

24. Sally Jones does an inservice on QI. To measure student learning as a result of her seminar, she gives a pre-test and post-test to the participants. The t-test she performs to determine statistical significance is a t-test of _____ means.

    A. dependent
    B. independent
    C. individual
    D. group

25. When variation is inherent in a process and a reduction of that variation is desired, what type of variance must be identified to eliminate tampering with the process?

    A. Common cause
    B. Root cause
    C. Special cause
    D. Variability cause

KEY (CORRECT ANSWERS)

#	Ans	#	Ans
1.	B	11.	A
2.	D	12.	A
3.	A	13.	A
4.	A	14.	D
5.	A	15.	A
6.	C	16.	D
7.	B	17.	B
8.	A	18.	D
9.	C	19.	B
10.	C	20.	C

21. A
22. A
23. D
24. A
25. B

TEST 3

DIRECTIONS: Each question or incomplete statement is followed by several suggested answers or completions. Select the one that BEST answers the question or completes the statement. *PRINT THE LETTER OF THE CORRECT ANSWER IN THE SPACE AT THE RIGHT.*

1. *Whenever a quality problem has multiple causes, just a few of those causes account for most of the incidents* is an expression of

   A. Deming's first principle
   B. Deming's third precept
   C. the Pareto principle
   D. the quality improvement principle

   1.____

2. The limits of a control chart for CQI are typically _____ standard deviation(s).

   A. one   B. two   C. three   D. four

   2.____

3. A chart that documents the mean is called a(n) _____ chart.

   A. x-bar   B. s-bar   C. r-bar   D. p-

   3.____

4. Following implementation of a QI initiative, which of the following tools would probably best answer the question, *Are we doing better*?

   A. Run chart
   B. Control chart
   C. Cause-and-effect diagram
   D. Histogram

   4.____

5. Which of the following are true regarding the granting of *locum tenens* privileges?
   I. Granted for a defined time period
   II. Granted after verifying minimal criteria
   III. Same as temporary privileges
   The CORRECT answer is:

   A. I, II   B. I, III   C. II, III   D. I, II, III

   5.____

6. If requested by the director of a clinical service, a CEO may grant temporary privileges to a physician upon
   I. verifying license and registration
   II. verifying current competency
   III. querying the National Practitioner Databank
   The CORRECT answer is:

   A. I, II   B. I, III   C. II, III   D. I, II, III

   6.____

7. A bar chart that does not provide the ordering of a Pareto chart would be called a

   A. run chart
   B. control chart
   C. cause-and-effect diagram
   D. histogram

   7.____

8. Which of the following statements are consistent with a focus on continuity of care?

   A. The same level of care is provided throughout the care setting.
   B. If nurses give injections on the floor, nurses should also be responsible for giving injections in radiology.
   C. Floor nurses should accompany their patients throughout the hospital.
   D. All of the above

9. If level 1 is the lowest level of understanding the needs of customers, and level 3 is the highest, which of the following is most likely to bring about a level 3 understanding?

   A. Unsolicited complaints
   B. Telephone hotline
   C. Focus groups
   D. All of the above

10. St. Joseph's Hospital finds that it receives different results on its patient satisfaction surveys on patients who are discharged in the evening, as compared to those discharged in the morning. This is an example of a(n)

    A. environmental contaminant
    B. reliability variation
    C. validity deficit
    D. response-set bias

11. The JCAHO defines _____ as *individuals permitted by law and healthcare organizations to provide patient care services without direction and supervision.*

    A. licensed independent practitioners
    B. licensed physicians
    C. licensed chiropractors
    D. registered nurses

12. Which of the following would be important *breakdowns* of data regarding CVA mortality?
    I. Death by cause; e.g., intracerebral hemorrhage, cerebral artery occlusion
    II. Death within 8 hours of admission
    III. Patient age

    The CORRECT answer is:

    A. I, II
    B. I, III
    C. II, III
    D. I, II, III

13. The reproducibility of measures on a survey indicates

    A. reliability
    B. construct validity
    C. content validity
    D. criterion validity

14. The greatest reliability in a measure of central tendency is found in the

    A. mean
    B. median
    C. mode
    D. standard deviation

15. If one is interested in whether cases fall only within upper and lower halves of the distribution and not how far from the central point, the _____ is calculated.

    A. mean
    B. median
    C. mode
    D. standard deviation

16. If one wants to determine the most typical case, the _____ is calculated.

    A. mean
    B. median
    C. mode
    D. standard deviation

17. If interpretations about the normal distribution curve are needed, the _____ is calculated.

    A. mean
    B. median
    C. mode
    D. standard deviation

18. What tests one or more hypotheses indicating that the means of all groups sampled come from populations with equal means, differing only because of sampling error?

    A. Standard deviation
    B. Range
    C. Simple correlation
    D. Analysis of variance

19. The best example of a morbidity review is the number of

    A. deaths following admission
    B. deaths due to gunshot wounds
    C. deaths due to nosocomial infections
    D. patients bedridden due to falls

20. A hospital QI committee feels that many delays in service, and subsequent extended patient stays, are due to the facts that radiology services are not delivered in a timely fashion. This is best verified through a(n) _____ review.

    A. admissions
    B. continued-stay
    C. department-specific
    D. observation bed

21. Range/6 is approximately equal to _____ standard deviation(s) when the sample size is approximately 100.

    A. one   B. two   C. four   D. six

22. Process measures (professional performance) are of most use when

    A. an accepted standard of care exists
    B. technology is effective
    C. patient variables (level of illness, age, etc.) are controlled
    D. all of the above

23. Adjusting for differences in case mix and case complexity is called

    A. outcomes analysis
    B. epidemiology
    C. risk adjustment
    D. risk management

24. Standards that reflect the best practices of medicine are called

    A. institutional
    B. empirical
    C. absolute (normative)
    D. internal

25. The most direct customer of a requisition for a chest x-ray generated by the admissions desk of a hospital would be the

    A. patient
    B. staff technologist
    C. chief technologist
    D. physician

KEY (CORRECT ANSWERS)

1. C
2. C
3. A
4. A
5. B

6. D
7. D
8. A
9. C
10. A

11. B
12. D
13. A
14. A
15. B

16. C
17. D
18. D
19. D
20. C

21. A
22. D
23. C
24. C
25. B

TEST 4

DIRECTIONS: Each question or incomplete statement is followed by several suggested answers or completions. Select the one that BEST answers the question or completes the statement. *PRINT THE LETTER OF THE CORRECT ANSWER IN THE SPACE AT THE RIGHT.*

1. Quality assurance is most synonymous with which of the following terms related to quality?   1.____

   A. Conformance quality
   B. Quality of kind
   C. Requirements quality
   D. Total quality

2. In CQI, the causes of a problem are determined based on   2.____

   A. intuition
   B. customer opinion
   C. empirical data
   D. management's decision

3. Which of the following statements is most appropriate for a quality goal?   3.____

   A. Quality is our most important product.
   B. This year we will work to improve our customers' satisfaction.
   C. No one will leave our department dissatisfied.
   D. During this quarter, we will reduce patient waiting time to no more than 10 minutes after arrival in the department.

4. Crosby was a proponent of which of the following ideas?   4.____

   A. *Zero defects* is the only performance standard
   B. The costs of quality are less than the losses of nonquality
   C. Conform to requirements to perform a task correctly on the first try
   D. All of the above

5. Approximately how long does it take for an organization to transform itself by implementing CQI techniques?   5.____

   A. 6 months   B. 1 year   C. 5 years   D. 10 years

6. In healthcare organizations, medical specialization adversely affects which of the following essential components of CQI?   6.____

   A. Knowledge
   B. Commitment
   C. Communication
   D. Patience

7. The cost of waste and nonconformance in the healthcare system has been estimated to be _____ of total costs associated with healthcare.   7.____

   A. less than 10%
   B. 20% to 40%
   C. 55% to 60%
   D. over 75%

8. A process owner is a member of a CQI team who   8.____
       I. supports the improvement process
       II. hinders the improvement process
       III. holds an upper level administrative position
   The CORRECT answer is:

   A. I, II   B. I, III   C. III *only*   D. I, II, III

177

9. A new neurosurgeon moves into a town with one hospital. The hospital refuses to grant him privileges. This physician might file a claim against the hospital based on _____ law.

   A. antitrust
   B. professional liability
   C. negligence
   D. ostensible agency

10. Written structure, process, and outcome criteria against which actual patient charts are screened to assess the adequacy of intervention efforts is known as

    A. audit
    B. critical pathways
    C. diagnosis related groups
    D. utilization review

11. All of the following characteristics are consistent with the CQI/TQM philosophy EXCEPT

    A. collective responsibilities
    B. accountability
    C. professional autonomy
    D. process expectations

12. The concept of benchmarking includes which of the following actions?

    A. Responding only as problems arise
    B. Changing based on the values of service providers
    C. Doing things the same way for a long time
    D. Comparing products and processes to those of the best competitor

13. Academic health centers do NOT

    A. set the standards for patient care
    B. educate most of the physicians in the United States
    C. conduct a significant portion of research that affects healthcare
    D. have little use of CQI due to structure

14. In the healthcare setting, the most significant conflict between management and practitioners involves

    A. the quality of clinical care
    B. relationships with patients
    C. cost reduction
    D. professional reputations

15. The BEST measure of team performance is

    A. quality of work products
    B. amount of time needed to solve the problem
    C. leader performance
    D. developing a large number of work products

16. Teams usually

    A. are ineffective
    B. outperform individuals acting alone
    C. provide minimal opportunity for advancement
    D. are not cost-effective

17. The optimal sequencing and timing of intervention best describes

   A. audit
   B. critical pathways
   C. diagnosis related groups
   D. utilization review

18. The range is BEST reported as a

   A. highest and lowest value
   B. difference
   C. percentage
   D. sum

19. Management influences team effectiveness by

   A. being directive
   B. demanding rapid solutions
   C. demonstrating the significance of the effort
   D. providing the team's work rules

20. The earliest known use of evaluating quality of clinical care by assessing patient outcomes was practiced by

   A. Deming
   B. Donabedian
   C. Codman
   D. Nightingale

21. Which of the following are components of a good team?

   A. A small number of individuals
   B. Individuals with complimentary skills
   C. Individuals with a common purpose
   D. All of the above

22. *Cooperating departments with the best intentions often lose sight of subtle slippage in effectiveness and efficiency.*
    Which of the following is related to this statement?

   A. Slippage is seen as an acceptable postimplementation adjustment
   B. Slippage can be reduced by a dedicated individual in the institution monitoring CQI efforts
   C. Periodic meetings with employees (team members) and managers are useful
   D. All of the above

23. Reducing average length of stay could be best accomplished with
    I. long-term purchase contracts
    II. developing critical pathways
    III. improving discharge planning
    The CORRECT answer is:

   A. I, II   B. I, III   C. II, III   D. I, II, III

24. A radiology manager wants to track x-ray repeat rate by room. Which of the following presentation strategies would probably offer the BEST presentation of the data for quick interpretation?

   A. Bar chart
   B. Pareto chart
   C. Pie chart
   D. Scatter diagram

25. A hospital with different conscious sedation strategies in different areas of the hospital (e.g., surgery, radiology) would NOT be recognizing the need for _____ of care. 25._____

   A. availability
   B. continuity
   C. efficacy
   D. timeliness

KEY (CORRECT ANSWERS)

1. A
2. C
3. D
4. D
5. D

6. C
7. B
8. A
9. A
10. A

11. C
12. D
13. D
14. C
15. A

16. B
17. B
18. A
19. C
20. D

21. D
22. D
23. C
24. B
25. B

GUIDE TO HEALTH CAREERS AND STRATEGY

TABLE OF CONTENTS

		Page
I.	Overview of the Health Field	1
	How many people work in the health industry?	1
	Who are the health support personnel?	1
	Who are these health workers?	2
	Where do these people work?	3
	Where will employment opportunities be?	6
	Changing opportunities from new technology	6
	New opportunities through expanded functions of some health workers	6
	Better opportunities in rural and inner-city communities	7
	More opportunities in primary care than in specialized care services	7
	Expanding opportunities in outpatient health facilities	7
	Opportunities for women and minorities	8
II.	Career Planning	8
	Health Careers: Something for everyone	8
	Exploring health careers	9
	Preparing for a health career	11
	Selecting a school for training	12
III.	Health Careers Calendar	14

GUIDE TO HEALTH CAREERS AND STRATEGY

I. Overview of the Health Field

If you could travel back in time about a hundred years, you would be surprised at how primitive health care was compared with what it is today. Those were the days of horse and buggy medicine when doctors often traveled long miles on country roads to treat their patients. Most medical care, from surgery to childbirth, took place in patients' homes rather than in hospitals. In 1873, there were only 178 hospitals in the entire country. Much of the medical treatment then was educated guesswork. In making a diagnosis, doctors had to depend solely on what their patients told them and what they could observe. No X-rays, lab tests, or advanced medical technologies were available to assist them. And once the problem was determined, there were no miracle drugs with which to treat patients. Even penicillin, a drug we take much for granted today, has been in general use only since World War II.

It is not surprising that the average life expectancy in 1900 was only 47.3 years, and diseases such as tuberculosis and diphtheria (which seldom occur today) were common killers.

The health system, what there was of it, was composed almost entirely of just three types of health workers-doctors, dentists, and nurses. Since the turn of the century, health care-like the world around us-has changed dramatically.

Today people seldom receive medical care in their own homes. The horse and buggy which carried doctors to patients has been replaced by the ambulance. Modern medicine has helped to increase the average life span to almost 80 years, and sophisticated technology assists doctors in the diagnosis, treatment, and prevention of illnesses. Within a short time, physicians can have a complete chemical analysis of body tissues and fluids. Computerized X-ray techniques make it possible to view entire cross sections of the human body, and the electron microscope can reveal to scientists even the molecular structure of a person's cells.

Health care has grown into a complex system with many important links. In this chapter, we will look briefly at some of the major links which are a part of the health care system. We will also examine some of the factors which are affecting the system today. Understanding where this system is now and where it might be going should give you extremely important clues to career opportunities. The chapter will not only help you evaluate where the jobs are likely to be but also show you where a particular health career fits into the entire picture.

- Americans see physicians over a billion times each year.
- Americans see dentists over 333 million times each year.
- One out of every 10 Americans goes to a hospital for care at least once during each year.

How Many People Work in the Health Industry?
- There are about 9 million people working in health care occupations as doctors, nurses, technicians, therapists and technologists.
- At least another million work as health support personnel in the maintenance and clerical staff found in health facilities; thousands more are employed as manufacturers of drugs or other health supplies.
- Many believe that the health industry will be the largest employer in our country within the next 10 years.

Who Are the Health Support Personnel?

These individuals have not been specifically trained in health, but their skills and knowledge are vital to daily operations. These professionals have chosen employment in the health field rather than in another industry. Almost any kind of worker who is found in business and other industries has a counterpart in health. Some of these workers are:

Accountant
Food Production Manager
Administrative Assistant
Bookkeeper
Cafeteria Manager
Cashier
Chaplain
Clerk (Accounts Payable and Receivable, Collection, File, General Office, Information, Insurance, Inventory, Mail, or Payroll)
Computer Operator
Controller-Business Manager
Credit Manager
Education Coordinator
Electronic Data Processing Manager
Employment Interviewer
Employment Supervisor
Executive Housekeeper

Food Production Manager
General Secretary
Job Analyst
Laundry Manager
Management Engineer
Personnel Director
Public Relations Director
Purchasing Agent
Receptionist
Stenographer
Stock Clerk
Stockroom Manager
Switchboard Operator
Systems Analyst
Training Coordinator
Typist
Wage and Salaray Administrator

Who Are These Health Workers?

Estimated number of people employed in selected health occupations

	Approximate Number	Percent of Total
Nursing	4,641,600	102.4
Medicine [1]	1,319,600	28.24
Dentistry	596,600	12.4
Health Services Administration	496,400	10.10
Clinical Laboratory Service	345,000	6.16
Pharmacy	265,800	4.18
Technical Instrumentation	265,000	4.18
Therapists	246,500	4.14
Science and Engineering	222,200	4.8
Dietetics and Nutrition	205,400	4.6
Health Information and Communication	161,600	2.16
Vision Care	119400	2.6
Psychology	75,000	.16
Veterinary Medicine	67,000	.14
Education	46,000	.10
Chiropractice	33,200	.8
	9,064,150 [2]	200.00

[1] Medicine includes, Physician, Podiatrist, Podiatric Assistant, Physician's Assistant, Medical Assistant, Emergency Medicial Technician, and Operating Room Technician.

[2] Not included in these figures are approximately 300,000 general secretarial and office workers who work in health facilities

Where Do These People Work?
Hospitals

Hospitals are the best known and largest single employer of health workers. In the broadest sense, hospitals can be grouped into two types—the general or short-term hospital and the specialty or long-term care facility.

The general hospital cares for the patients with varying medical conditions which require diagnosis and surgical/medical treatment. This is the hospital you are most likely to see in your own community and to go to if you or a member of your family has a medical problem. They represent 87 percent of all hospitals. Patients in these hospitals generally stay a short time-a few days to a few weeks.

In specialty hospitals, patients are usually limited to those who have a specific illness or condition. Some of these hospitals are for psychiatric, chronic disease, and rehabilitation patients. Specialty hospitals are also identified generally as "long-term," since their patients are usually hospitalized for several months before they are well enough to return to their homes.

Both specialty and general hospitals may vary in size. Some may have as few as 50 hospital beds while others may have well over 1,000 beds.

Also, hospitals are identified by their ownership: Government, voluntary, and proprietary hospitals.

Government hospitals may be operated and supported by cities, States, or the Federal Government. A city or municipal hospital, a State psychiatric Institution, or a Veterans Administration hospital is examples of government institutions.

The voluntary hospitals are nonprofit institutions which are privately owned by religious or nonreligious groups.

Finally, proprietary hospitals are those which operate for profit. They are most often owned by a hospital chain corporation or a group of physicians. These hospitals are usually small and offer limited medical services.

Nursing Homes

Nursing homes were almost unknown before the 1930's; however, since then the number of them has grown rapidly. Today we have over 30,000 nursing homes which employ over one million people. Depending on the individual nursing home, the services offered may vary from skilled bedside nursing to simple personal care (bathing, dressing, providing meals, etc.). Though nursing homes are associated with the elderly, adults of any age who are victims of certain diseases or accidents may require nursing home care.

Other Inpatient Facilities

In addition to nursing homes, there are over 5,000 other residential health facilities for persons who do not necessarily have to be hospitalized. These include residential schools or homes for the mentally retarded, emotionally disturbed, physically handicapped, the deaf, the blind, dependent children, alcoholics, and drug abusers. About half of these facilities are for the mentally retarded and emotionally disturbed and employ about three-quarters of the 250,000 workers in this type of institution.

Outpatient and Other Health Facilities or Services

Close to half a million health workers are employed in other vital types of settings or services which are often overlooked as part of the health industry when evaluating career opportunities in the health fields.

1. *Ambulance Services*—transport patients and frequently provide emergency medical services.

2. *Blood Banks*—draw, process, store, and distribute human whole blood and its derivatives.

3. *Clinical (Medical) Laboratories*—test samples of tissues or fluids to determine the presence and extent or absence of diseases in order to help physicians diagnose or treat illness.

4. *Dental Laboratories*—provide services to dentists by making and repairing artificial teeth and other dental appliances.

5. *Family Planning Services*—provide physican examinations, laboratory tests, consultations, treatments, and issuance of drugs and contraceptives related to reproduction.

6. *Home Health Services*—provide health care and supportive services to sick or disabled persons at their place of residence when the nature of their illness does not require hospital or nursing home care or when their disabilities do not allow them to travel to an outpatient health facility

7. *Optician Establishments*—stores or shops that sell and/or make eyeglasses according to the prescription of an optometrist or an ophthalmologist.

8. *Poison Control Centers*—provide information on the ingredients of poisons and recommend treatment. Some centers also have facilities for treating poison victims.

9. *Rehabilitation Centers*—provide comprehensive services for people with physical, mental, or social disabilities to help them return to a satisfying job and lifestyle. Certain centers might work with special problems only-rehabilitation of the blind, the deaf, or the mentally retarded.

10. *Community Mental Health Centers*—provide inpatient/outpatient, day care, 24-hour emergency, consultation, and educational services for problems related to mental health.

11. *Migrant Health Programs*—provide health services to migrant and seasonal farmworkers who would not ordinarily qualify for health services available to permanent residents of a particular State.

12. *Neighborhood Health Centers*—provide medical, dental, laboratory, radiological, and pharmaceutical services for people living in a particular geographic area within a city.

13. *Health Maintenance Organizations (HMO)*—provide consumers with comprehensive health services including hospitalization, office visits, preventive health checkups, and immunizations. Instead of the traditional pay-as-yougo system, consumers and/or their employers pay a fixed monthly fee which covers all these services no matter how often they are used.

14. *Government*—at the Federal, State and local level offers numerous opportunities for health professionals. State and local governments operate health departments which

help to control the spread of communicable diseases, safeguard the purity of food and water supplies, and promote health education and health measures such as inoculations.

In the Federal Government, The U. S. Department of Health, Education, and Welfare"s Public Health Services (PHS) is specifically concerned with the health of all Americans.

Other branches of the Government also offer opportunities for health-related employment. The U.S. Department of Labor's Occupational Safety and Health Administration enforces standards related to job health and safety. The U.S. Department of Agriculture's State-sponsored programs insure that the meat, poultry, and eggs we eat are disease free and meet sanitary conditions. The U.S. Army, Navy, and Air Force and the Veterans Administration offer employment opportunities in just about every health occupation described in this book.

15. *Health Practitioners' Offices*—employ health professionals of various kinds, depending on the size of the practice and the patients who are being served. Some practitioners work alone in private practice while others "group" together and share office space and services. This is called a group practice. Practitioners who commonly operate their own offices include medical and osteopathic physicians, dentists, chiropractors, podiatrists, optometrists, psychologists, and veterinarians.

16. *Voluntary Health Agencies*—at the national, State, and local levels are concerned with specific health problems or health services. Some of their activities include raising funds for medical research, alerting the public to specific health problems, providing health education programs, and making health services more available at a community level. The American Cancer Society, The National Foundation-March Of Dimes, The American National Red Cross, and the American Heart Association are examples of voluntary health agencies.

17. *Professional Health Associations*—at the national, State, and local levels represent the members of a particular health profession or of a particular type of health facility such as an association of hospJtals or community health centers. Their activities often include improving the professional education of their members, establishing standards of practice or operations for their fields, and carrying out research of interest to their members. The American Medical Association, American Hospital Association, American Association of Medical Assistants, and the National Association of Community Health Centers are some examples.

18. *Industry*—not only manufactures prescription drugs and numerous over-the-counter medications but also produces common household health supplies as well as supplies used by hospitals and other health facilities.

Medical devices such as hearing aids, cardiac pacemakers, artificial limbs, and braces are made by industry, as is the sophisticated diagnostic and treatment equipment used by health personnel today.

But industry does not just produce these items; it also employs thousands of people in research and development to discover new health products and technology which will improve health care.

Because industry employs millions of people, many of the large corporations have started health clinics manned by health professionals within their own companies. Here employees can receive immediate, on-the-spot health care as well as health checkups. Occupational health and safety of workers is a vital concern, and industry employs special health personnel to insure that employees will not be exposed to unnecessary job hazards.

Occupational health and safety of workers is a vital concern, and industry employs special health personnel to insure that employees will not be exposed to unnecessary job hazards.

Where Will Employment Opportunities Be?

Health care is always moving in new and different directions. These directions may alter what health workers will be doing, where they will be working, and how many will be employed in a particular occupation. Opportunities may expand in some areas and diminish in others. This has already happened in the case of many careers described in the occupational briefs included in this publication.

No one can predict with absolute certainty what the future employment outlook will be for a particular career. The following trends will give you some clues as to where you might find especially good opportunities today and in the future.

Changing Opportunities from New Technology

Advances in technology are frequently responsible for many changes. Research is constantly conducted to discover methods of preventing disease or to improve ways of diagnosing and treating illness. This often results in the development and introduction of a complex machine or a sophisticated medical technique into health care. Of course, when this happens, health workers must be trained to operate the machine or to perform the technique correctly and safely.

The first persons selected for training are usually people who are already employed in health and work in a related area. They receive on-the-job training. However, as the new service becomes better known and is more widely used by hospitals and other health facilities, more workers are needed. On-the-job training is often no longer practical, and formal education programs in hospitals or colleges are started. Qualified students—not just health care workers—then have the opportunity for training. As the number of these newly trained workers increases, a separate and distinct new occupation may emerge.

New Opportunities Through Expanded Functions of Some Health Workers

The work of the dental hygienist is a case in point. The daily work activities of this health professional have been expanded. That is, dental hygienists in many States now perform some tasks which were previously done by dentists alone. These increased responsibilities have resulted from a new understanding of how overall dental care can be provided. We realize now that dental hygienists; with additional careful training, can safely perform some activities performed by dentists such as giving local anesthetics. This frees dentists to carry out the more complicated procedures for which their extensive training has prepared them. It also means that the dentist, assisted by a dental hygienist, can provide dental services to more patients without sacrificing the quality of dental care.

This same concept is being used in medical care today with the physician assistant and nurse practitioner. Both of these professionals perform many of the tasks which were traditionally only done by physicians. Giving physical examinations, prescribing simple medications, and giving immunizations or patient treatments are some of the tasks they perform. Physicians can then devote their time to patients who are more seriously ill.

Better Opportunities in Rural and Inner-City Communities

.Today in some parts of the country new health workers are finding it difficult to obtain jobs, while in other places communities cannot find enough of the same people to fill existing jobs. This is a national problem often referred to as the maldistribution of health personnel. It means that health care workers are not distributed according to the population~' size, and health needs of many geographic areas. Over-populated inner-city areas and underpopulated rural areas are hardest hit by this maldistribution.

In 1993, 140 rural counties were without a practicing physician. In the poverty areas of Chicago, there were 26 physicians for 100,000 residents, while in its more affluent areas there were 210 physicians for every 100,000 people. Doctors are not the only health workers who are in short' supply. Shortage areas need health professionals of all kinds. All this means is that you might have to relocate to where you are most needed in order to find the best future opportunities.

More Opportunities in Primary Care Than in Specialized Care Services

Most Americans need primary health care which focuses on prevention, early detection and treatment, and continued overall responsibility for the patient. Primary care can often reduce health costs, since it is generally easier and cheaper to prevent problems or treat them in their earliest stages. Although the number of primary care physicians is growing, physicians who practice this kind of basic medicine are still outnumbered 3 to 1 by those doctors who specialize in other fields.

Primary care services should become increasingly more available. Medical schools are encouraging students to go into primary care practice by emphasizing its importance and by exposing students to primary care earlier in their training. Primary care is now even recognized as an official medical specialty under the name of "family medicine"-comprehensive, primary health care services for all family members.

This increased emphasis on primary care affects not only the career of the physician but also of most other health workers who assist or support the physician. Where people work is also affected. Facilities which emphasize primary care, such as health maintenance organizations and neighborhood health centers, should increase in number.

Expanding Opportunities in Outpatient Health Facilities

Just 20 years ago the United States spent $40 billion on health care. Today we spend well over $1 trillion. Containing these costs will be a major, if not the most important, priority of the health field during the coming years.

Because the cost of inpatient care in hospitals and nursing homes represents a large part of our Nation's health care bill, new efforts have been taken to keep this cost down. Outpatient alternatives to hospitals or nursing homes are being used successfully. Home care services now enable many ill or aged people to remain in their own homes rather than live as patients in nursing homes. With a growing elderly population, home care services should become increasingly more important and again more persons will be needed to deliver these services.

Ambulatory or "walk-in" patient care in private practitioners' offices, hospital outpatient departments, community health centers, or other health facilities is helping to reduce hospitalization.

In the past, many medical procedures, including certain diagnostic tests and simple surgery, were only done on an inpatient hospital basis. Now, however, these same procedures are safely and routinely performed on an outpatient basis in an office setting. This greater emphasis on ambulatory care may shift employment opportunities from hospitals to other kinds of health facilities.

Opportunities for Women and Minorities

In recent years thousands of women and minorities have entered health professions in which they have traditionally been underrepresented. The following enrollment figures from medical schools are an example of the fact that many of them are now saying "yes, I can" to such fields:

Women and minorities as a percent of all first-year medical students

	1968-69	2008-09
Women.	9.0	22.2
Minorities.	4.2	12.5

Increases can be seen in the other professions where these groups have been traditionally underrepresented such as dentist, veterinarian, optometrist, podiatrist, and health services administrator. However, these in-creases have only touched the surface of the need and opportunity for women and minorities in such careers.

Women who represent over 50 percent of the population still represent less than 12 percent of all physicians, dentists, and optometrists. Blacks represent about 11 percent of the population. However, less than 3 percent of our physicians, dentists, optometrists, and pharmacists are black. Blacks, Hispanics, and American Indians represent just over 1 percent of all dentists and optometrists.

To correct this underrepresentation, Congress, Federal and State agencies, and professional associations in the health field are making special efforts to create new educational and job opportunities for women and minorities in these fields.

The trends discussed are not the only ones in health care today. But they may begin to make you aware of what's happening in the health field. So while you look into your future as a health worker, watch carefully the health care system. Be alert to the changes and advances that are reported in newspapers and television today. They may affect how and where you become involved in the health field and may help to guide your future.

II. Career Planning
Health Careers:
Something for Everyone

The health field, perhaps more than any other career area, offers wide-ranging opportunities which can match almost any interest.

Do you like to work with your hands? Dental technicians, optical mechanics, biomedical equipment technicians, prosthetists, and many other health professionals work with their hands.

Are you interested in working with machines? Respiratory therapists, electroencephalograph (EEG) technologists, and radiologic technologists are just a few professionals who work with patients and medical machines.

Are you fascinated by photography or the fine arts? Art, music, or dance therapist or biological photographer are among the health careers where you can use these talents.

Do you enjoy working with people? Nursing, medicine, dentistry, optometry, social work, rehabilitation, and mental health are some health careers areas that will give you the opportunity to work with, and help, peorle of all ages.

These careers only scratch the surface of possibilities. Health careers really offer something for everyone; but, too often, students say "no" to health careers simply because they don't have the real facts.

Could you fall into this trap? Let's see. Below are some common statements students make when talking about health careers.

"I couldn't work around sick people in a hospital. That's depressing. Besides I can't stand the sight of blood."

A health career doesn't automatically mean a hospital job or care of the sick. Health careers have many facets. You can work in health care in research, health planning and administration, health education, disease prevention, environmental protection, and other important areas.

Jobs are not just in hospitals. Private doctors' offices, schools, government, industry, and many other places need and employ health workers, too. But don't judge hospital work until you try it-either as a hospital volunteer or as a part-time employee. You may discover by working there and observing trained health professionals, you, too, can learn to accept the less pleasant parts of helping people get well as a fact of life.

You'll also find that even in hospitals many jobs are "behind-the-scene" with little or no direct contact with patients.

"You need science and math for health careers. That's not for me."

Sure, science and math are required for some health care jobs but many don't require or emphasize these subjects. Health education, social services, and mental health are just a few areas where psychology, social studies, and other subjects are stressed. But even when science and math are needed, different levels of skills are required. Some career occupations like optometrists and scientists require indepth knowledge while many other careers require just good basic skills and working knowledge of these subjects.

"Training takes too long."

Yes, some careers do take 7 or more year's preparation after high school. But most require only 2 to 4 years' preparation-not a very big investment considering that most people work over 40 years in their lifetime. But 2 to 4 years is just an average: Some can be learned in less than 2 years' training, some even on the job. The Health Careers Calendar on page 25 will give you a quick picture of training time for many careers.

"Training costs too much."

In one sense, cost is only relative. It must be balanced against what you can earn. Figures show that lifetime earnings generally increase with years of education. On the other hand, if you don't think you can afford training, you're not alone. Most students today need financial aid for training. The Financial Aid chapter (p.15) will give you the facts.

"The training is too hard."

Don't sell yourself short. Many students who felt the same way are now working as doctors, nurses, therapists, technologists, or as other health professionals. If you think training may be too hard for you, because you've not been doing well enough in school, then think twice. A change of attitude, a special remedial program, or additional study may be all you need to succeed. You might discover by trying that health careeers training is like learning anything new. It can be difficult at first but with time and effort, it is possible.

Exploring Health Careers

Career exploration is a real learning experience. You don't have to make any definite career decision. Instead you make new discoveries about yourself and the world of work.

While you're exploring, learn as much as possible about each health occupation. Find out: Where, how, and why the health worker performs this kind of work? What skills and knowledge does he or she needs? What is the work setting like? Does the job involve working alone or with others? What are the minimum job requirements in this profession? Is licensure, professional certification, or registration a factor in gaining employment? How much does the job pay? What are the advancement possibilities? Finally, what is the job picture where you live and elsewhere in the country?

How do you start exploring health careers? That's easy. You've already started just by reading about health careers. But don't stop here. The information in this book is just the tip of the iceberg. Read more about health careers. Visit your school or public library. Write to the professional health organizations listed in this book and to the schools that provide training for health occupations.

The information you'll get from books and pamphlets can be very helpful, but it's no substitute for your own firsthand investigation. This requires one special ingredient-you. You must now explore by doing. Investigate your health career potential by trying these activities:

Visit a hospital, laboratory, or other health facility. Most institutions welcome the opportunity to show their facilities to interested students and the community-atlarge. Some may schedule regular guided tours; others may offer these by special appointment. A hospital tour, for example, will give you a good overall picture of the many different departments and jobs which are part of medical care. You'll also learn about the hospital's special services and programs and how it helps the community. You can arrange to visit a health facility by contacting the Director of Public Relations or the Office of the Administrator.

Visit health occupations schools. Like health facilities, most schools offer tours or hold open house days where you can meet teachers and students, find out more about the profession, what training involves, and the necessary entrance requirements. Some schools even permit prospective students to spend a day on campus, attend classes, and get a special preview of student life. The admissio'1s office of the school should be contacted to make the necessary arrangements.

Talk to health professionals and students in health training. You'll receive a special outlook on the career and obtain information you won't find in any book. Ask them: How did they get interested in and choose their particular field? How difficult is the training? What happens during a typical student day or workday? What do they like most-and least-about their chosen profession? You can meet health professionals and students through exploring many of the activities described here. Your family doctor, school nurse, or guidance teacher may also be able to assist you.

Work in a health facility or agency. A part-time or summer job in a hospital, nursing home, laboratory, other health facility, or agency can give you intensive, first-hand experience. Generally you will have an opportunity to observe trained health professionals in action and perform simple tasks. Start your job hunt by making a list of potential health employers, then contact the Director of Personnel of each facility or agency. Find out whether they hire part-time or summer-student help and, if so, how can you qualify. Summer jobs are often hard to obtain so it's important to contact potential employer's early-several months before the summer season.

Volunteer in a health facility or agency. It's not always possible to get a job but almost everyone can volunteer. Generally the only requirements are that you have some free time (3 or 4 hours per week) and are interested in helping others. Hospitals, nursing homes, social service agencies, correctional institutions, and day care or senior citizen centers are among the places where volunteers can be found. Unlike a job where specific work is assigned, volunteer positions are flexible. Every effort is made to assign volunteers to areas of their choice. In general, volunteers provide services which support or compliment those of the paid staff. They do not substitute for regular workers.

What exactly does a volunteer do? That depends on the policy of the individual institution. In hospitals, volunteers assist patients and staff by providing those special extras for which regular staff may not have time. Some examples of volunteer positions are:

- Patient escort: Help transport patients from one area of a hospital to another

- Friendly visitor: Spend time talking to patients, making them feel more at home, perhaps reading to them or writing letters for them
- Messenger: Carry messages for staff from one department to another
- Department aide: Help staff wherever assistance is needed. On a nursing floor this may mean answering a patient's call light and relaying the patient's needs to the nurse in charge. In the Recreation Department, a volunteer might organize and lead a small patient group in a game or other activity.

Volunteers do these tasks and more. New work assignments in both patient and nonpatient areas are constantly being developed to meet the hospitals' needs and the individual interests of their volunteers.

If you'd like to become a volunteer, contact the Director of Volunteer Services of the health facility or agency in which you're interested. He or she can tell you what volunteers generally do at the institution and if there are special requirements. Don't be afraid to let the Volunteer Director know which health careers you're interested in exploring. With this information the director can make a good assignment for you.

Join health career clubs or programs. Many schools and community organizations sponsor activities which allow you to explore health occupations. The Girl Scouts, Boy Scouts, and Explorers all have special health career programs. Many secondary and postsecondary schools have a career club. If your school doesn't, you can help start one. Some high schools have prevocational health occupations programs. There is even a national student organization for students enrolled in these programs called the Health Occupations Students of America (HOSA).

To find out whether any of the above activities are going on in your school or community, check with the guidance department, the school nurse, or student health service.

While you're exploring, too, keep an open mind. Investigate many careers, not only those with which you're familiar. Remember the more information you get now, the better your career decisions will be later.

Each year many interested and qualified students give up on a health career simply because they have not explored alternate choices when their first career choice isn't possible. A prime example is the aspiring physician who is not admitted to a medical or an osteopathic school and drops the health field entirely.

The health field is vast; in it you'll find many related careers where you can contribute and find personal satisfaction. The health field doesn't want to lose your talents, so have other options ready.

Preparing for a Health Career

Whether you realize it or not, you are preparing for your health career right now. Your high school provides the foundation upon which later health occupations training will build.

Even if you haven't chosen a particular career yet, you can still prepare. You can't go wrong taking courses which will improve communications skills like English and writing and courses which will build reading speed and comprehension. If you're considering a scienceoriented or patient-care career, take laboratory sciences and mathematics courses, too. These subjects are routinely required in these areas.

Depending on the profession(s) you are considering, a high school diploma, some college, or a college degree will be needed before you begin your training. But regardless of how. much preprofessional education is required, the same rules apply: Contact the schools which offer programs for your health profession early. (Most health professions organizations can provide you with a school list). Find out what specific courses are required for admission; then take those courses.

If you are still in high school and are considering a career where graduate school education is necessary, it's still important to contact the professional schools early. This information will help you choose high school courses that will give you a good foundation for your undergraduate education. It will also guide you in later selecting a preprofessional curriculum in college.

Competition for admission to most health careers training is keen. Grades definitely count. Good grades now in all your courses, but particularly in those required for admission will pay off later-when you face that competition.

Selecting a School for Training

Next to choosing a career, selecting a school for training is the most important career decision you'll have to make. As you read the job requirements in this Guidebook you'll discover that health careers training is available in many different kinds of schools: 2-year and 4-year colleges and universities, technical institutes, medical, dental, or other professional schools, hospitals, private vocational, or trade schools, and the military. The challenge, of course, is to choose the school that's best for you.

The secret to selecting the right school is tied to one important question: Will the school you are interested in prepare you for the career you want? Before you seek the answer to this question, you should understand three basic terms related to employment in the health field:

Licensure: Before you can work in many health professions, a State license is required. The qualifications for licensure vary. In general, a student must graduate from a school whose program is *approved* by the State licensing agency, then prove he or she is qualified to give health services by passing a special licensing examination. Licensure is the State's way of protecting the public from unqualified health practitioners.

The health professions which are licensed vary with each State. Some professions like registered nurse, practical nurse, physician, dentist, optometrist, podiatrist, pharmacist, and veterinarian are licensed in all States. The individual State licensing agencies vary, too. The State Education Department, Department of Higher Education, or Department of Health are usually the responsible agencies. Licensing may also be done jointly by a State agency and a State specialty Board of Nursing, Dentistry, etc.

Professional certification: Professional certification insures that health professionals meet established levels of competency. Certification is granted by the national health professions organizations, not the individual States, so it has national recognition. In health professions where there is no State licensure, professional certification may be required for employment. But even when-not required, it is a strong employment asset. Most employers prefer to hire certified professionals, and in a tight job market certification may be the key to getting a job.

All health professions do not have certification programs. The occupational briefs in this book tell you if a career you are considering has professional certification.

In general, to qualify for certification, a student must first complete a program of training recognized by the profession. Usually this means graduating from a school whose program is accredited (approved) by the organization. Some organizations accredit programs jointly with the American Medical Association (AM A); then, the student must pass a special certification examination.

Professional Registration: Technically, registration means the listing of certified health professionals on an official roster kept by a State agency or health professions organization. In practical terms, some health professions organizations use "registration" interchangeably with "certification."

The licensure, certification, or registration necessary for each career is further discussed under "Job Requirements." If your profession is licensed, you must find out if you as a graduate of this school can qualify for that licensing examination. If certification or registration is required, can you as a graduate of this school qualify for certification or registration?

The State licensing agency and the health professions organizations can best answer this question. Both can provide you with a list of schools whose programs have been approved or accredited. If your school's program is not on that list, don't enroll. It can't prepare you for the job you want.

If licensure or certification is not required in your field, then you must take extra care to determine whether the school you are interested in will prepare you for the job you want.

Contact potential employers and ask: Would you hire graduates of this school? How many have you hired in the last year? Were they hired because of the school's training? Did training make any difference in their starting salary?

Talk to your high school counselor, a counselor at a State employment agency, and graduates of the school's program. (A reputable school will give you the names of graduates upon request.) See how they rate the school.

If possible, visit the school and evaluate the program carefully. How does it compare with its brochure? Is equipment actually available for technical courses? Is the equipment the kind currently used in health facilities or is it outdated? Is there enough equipment for students enrolled? If entering the profession requires clinical experience (supervised practice with patients or machines), find out what kind of experience the program offers. Experience in actual health facilities is always preferred; however, in many careers simulated classroom practice can be an acceptable substitute.

If the school you are interested in attending is a commercial, vocational, or trade school run for profit, the best way to evaluate the quality of the education you will receive is to follow the same guidelines just outlined for nonprofit schools, such as checking to see whether or not you will be able to meet licensure or certification requirements.

The U.S. Federal Trade Commission recommends that you take some extra steps. Call the Office of the Federal Trade Commission, Chamber of Commerce, or the Better Business Bureau for information about the school. Ask the school about its dropout and job placement rates. Check the school's refund policy should you decide to cancel or drop out. Finally, take the contract home and read it carefully before signing.

There are hundreds of excellent commercial schools that will give you the health career education you are seeking. Some may not. If the school does not measure up, don't take a chance with your future.

You may find that several of the schools you're interested in can prepare you for that career, but you may be undecided on which type of school-hospital, 2-year or 4-year college, etc., may be best for you. Each of these institutions may have a special advantage or drawback which you should consider before making your choice. The advice of the health professions organizations, potential employers, health professionals, and students will steer you in the right direction.

If you follow these guidelines, you are likely to find the school that is best for you. This takes time and work, but it's worth it.

After all, your school is where your future begins.

III. Health Careers Calandar

This calendar gives you a quick check on how many years of education, after high school, you should count on for the representative health occupations listed here. The lines and symbols show what is customary—some people take only minimum required training; many take more.

●   Requires no special training.

●··········   Entails an apprenticeship, special course, or on-the-job training.

▬▬▬▬   Requires special training in college, a hospital, special school, or a professional school after 1 to 4 years of college.

○   Though the line shows the minimum period to qualify, more preprofessional years in college lengthen the total training time.

□   First square means one can get a junior professional job after college. Subsequent squares indicate that more study—to or beyond the master's or doctor's degree—as well as experience is usually needed for advancement.

▬▬··········   Requires special training of varying periods of time.

This calendar pictures training information in condensed timetable form. To get a more detailed picture, read the *Health Careers Guidebook* Occupational Descriptions and consult your school advisers for information and personal guidance on training and the local outlook for the career you want.

Years of Education and Training Beyond High School For Careers in Health Occupations

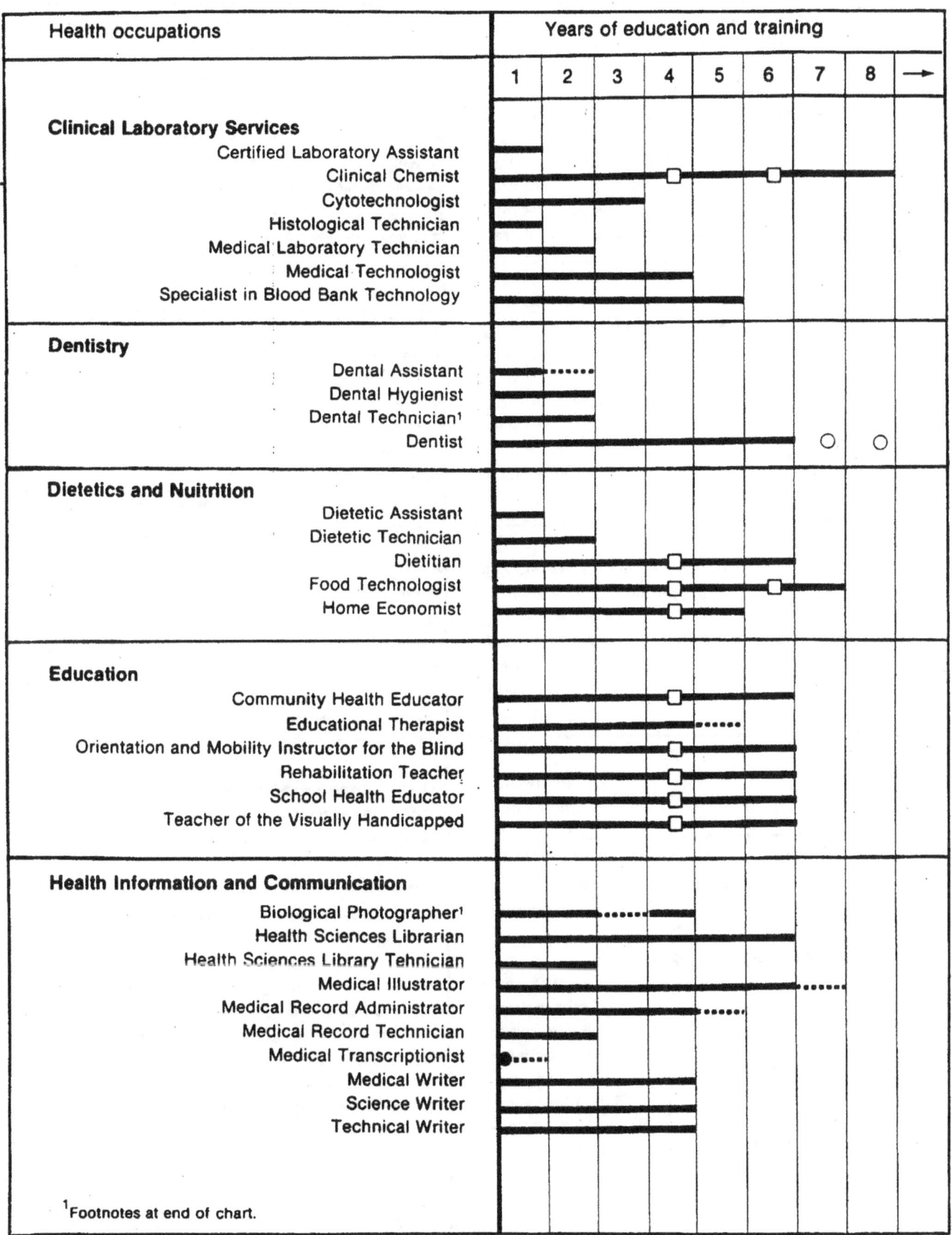

Years of Education and Training Beyond High School For Careers in Health Occupation--Continued

Health occupations	Years of education and training (1–8+)
Health Services Administration	
Executive Director, Voluntary Health Agency	1–6 (marker at 4)
Health Services Administrator	1–6
Hospital Administrator	1–6
Medical Secretary	1 (dotted to 2)
Nursing Home Administrator	1 (dotted 3–5)
Medicine	
Chiropractor	1–6
Emergency Medical Technician	• dotted to 2
Medical Assistant	1 (dotted to 2)
Operating Room Technician	1 (dotted to 2)
Osteopathic Physician	1–8+ (○)
Physician	1–8+ (○)
Physician Assistant	1–3
Podiatric Assistant	1
Podiatrist	1–6 (○ at 7, ○ at 8)
Nursing	
Homemaker-Home Health Aide	• dotted to 2
Licensed Practical Nurse	1–2
Nurse Anesthetist	1–3 (dotted 3–6)
Nurse Midwife	1–3 (dotted 3–5)
Nurse Practitioner	1–3 (dotted 3–6)
Nurse's Aide	• dotted to 2
Registered Nurse	1–3 (dotted 3–4)
Pharmacy	
Pharmacist	1–6 (○ 6, ○ 7, ○ 8)
Pharmacologist	1–6 (○ 6, ○ 7, ○ 8+)
Psychology	
Psychiatric/Mental Health Technician	1–2
Psychologist	1–7 (marker at 7)
Science and Engineering	
Anatomist	1–4 (□), 6 (□), extends 8+
Anthropologist	1–4 (□), 6 (□), extends 8+
Bacteriologist	1–4 (□), 6 (□), extends 8+
Biochemist	1–4 (□), 6 (□), extends 8+
Biologist	1–4 (□), 6 (□), extends 8+
Biomathematician	1–4 (□), 6 (□), extends 8+
Biomedical Engineer	1–4 (□)
Biomedical Equipment Technician	1–2 (dotted to 5)

Footnotes at end of chart.

Years of Education and Training Beyond High School For Careers in Health Occupations--Continued

Health occupations	Years of education and training								
	1	2	3	4	5	6	7	8	→

Science and Engineering (continued)
- Biophysicist
- Biostatistician
- Cryogenicist
- Ecologist
- Embryologist
- Entomologist
- Environmental Engineer
- Environmental Health Technician
- Epidemiologist
- Geneticist
- Health Physicist
- Hematologist
- Hydrophysicist
- Immunologist
- Industrial Hygienist
- Microbiologist
- Parasitologist
- Physiologist
- Radiobiologist
- Sanatarian
- Serologist
- Virologist

Social Work
- Clinical Social Worker
- Medical Social Worker
- Psychiatric Social Worker
- Social Service Assistant

Technical Instrumentation
- Cardiology Technologist/Technician
- Cardiopulmonary Technologist/Technician
- Diagnostic Medical Sonographer
- Dialysis Technician
- Electroencephalographic Technician
- Electroencephalographic Technologist
- Nuclear Medicine Technologist
- Perfusionist
- Radiation Therapy Technologist
- Radiologic Technologist
- Respiratory Therapist
- Respiratory Therapy Technician

Years of Education and Training Beyond High School For Careers in Health Occupations--Continued

Health occupations	Years of education and training								
	1	2	3	4	5	6	7	8	→

Therapists
- Art Therapist
- Athletic Trainer
- Corrective Therapist
- Dance Therapist
- Horticultural Therapist
- Manual Arts Therapists
- Music Therapist
- Occupational Therapist
- Occupational Therapy Assistant
- Orthotic-Prosthetic Technician
- Orthotist
- Physical Therapist
- Physical Therapist Assistant
- Prosthetist
- Recreation Therapist
- Speech Pathologist and Audiologist
- Vocational Rehabilitation Counselor

Veterinary Medicine
- Animal Technican
- Veterinarian

Vision Care
- Dispensing Optician
- Ophthalmic Medical Assistant
- Optical Laboratory Technician
- Optometric Assistant
- Optometric Technician
- Optometrist
- Orthoptist